The Don

Scottish Lowlands Hills 610m or above

By Elizabeth Layhe

This book is dedicated to Ken, my husband and walking companion of many years.

Designed by Michael Johnston, Martins the Printers
Printed and bound in Britain by Martins the Printers
Published by Entire Productions

Acknowledgements

I would like to thank all who in any way, small or otherwise helped to make this book a reality. In particular to Ken Layhe, Alison McIntosh and Michael Johnston.

"To those who have never visited these hills any will repay the effort, although some accustomed to the higher hills of the North may view these as being commonplace and devoid of adventure. They have a solemn grandeur of their own with their round backed hills, vales and streams."

Pilkington

Contents

Preface

In 1978 on a rather misty October day a group of us travelled from Perth with the intention of trying out some hills in Galloway instead of the usual diet of Munros. We knew nothing of Donalds and would probably have instantly dismissed them if we had - how wrong we would have been.

These hills gave us a weekend of challenges, improved our navigational skills and impressed us by their isolation and remoteness. Never again would I reject anything lower than the magic 3,000 foot mark as being unworthy of being climbed.

The idea to walk these hills in the same order as Donald and in approximately the same number of days and time came after a few years of living in the Borders away from the giants of the North. The challenge was not so much the height but in the fact that they were classic walks giving long days over wild country. Since then I have walked these hills in various combinations and still enjoy them.

As more people turn to lower hills to seek solitude, more hills are defined and given names such as "Grahams" or "New Donalds". This is not what this book is about; instead it describes routes and walks in hills in Southern Scotland as defined by Percy Donald himself but which also lend themselves to long days in beautiful countryside.

The book is divided into sections based on the Donalds as tabled in "Munro's Tables and Other Tables of Lesser Heights" published by the S.M.C., this is merely for ease of reference. The sketch maps are only rough guides and it is recommended that Ordnance Survey maps be used when planning or following the routes. The complete walk distances are approximate. I have not given times as conditions can change and it can depend on how fit you are or how many people there are in the group. However a rough estimate would be to calculate 1 to 1 ½ minutes per contour line and approximately 4kph on horizontal ground.

The routes give long days over rough terrain and are for the fit with knowledge of map and compass, if at all uncertain then the routes can be shortened. I found them fun and a challenge giving some very long difficult days on one hand and a few short days on the other. I hope that you too will enjoy the challenge and fun of these great hills and that you travel safely and wisely.

Please note all maps are not to scale.

Elizabeth Layhe
November 2006

INTRODUCTION

THE IDEA AND THE MAN

At the back of the S.M.C. guide titled 'Munros's Tables' is a list of hills in the Scottish Lowlands of 2,000ft and above. There are 87 of them placed in twelve sections; the last section includes six hills in England. This list or table was the work of Percy Donald who meticulously worked out the height of each hill then visited them before issuing his list to the Scottish Mountaineering Club for publication.

Donald joined the Scottish Mountaineering Club in 1922 and served on the committee for three years. He was an experienced hill walker and regularly attended at the S.M.C. meets, but he often walked alone. In fact the idea to list the 2000ft hills in the Lowlands came to him when out on one of his many solitary expeditions.

His ambition was to complete the Lowland 2,000footers in winter within a time limit of a month. However, as he pointed out in his article in the S.M.C. journal this was impossible on account of the short days and chilly nights of December, but between the 12th December 1932 and the 28th May 1933 Donald had finished his self appointed task.

Donald lived in Edinburgh and based his method of transport on train or bus services from there, although on two occasions he got a lift by car to his starting point. These journeys were often in treacherous conditions when snow was at ground level and in one instance the small one man bus had no heater other than a rug! Very often bus time tables, daylight hours and weather caused problems.

Percy Donald was a man of extremely strong character with an eye for painstaking detail and therefore he enjoyed the challenge of neatly arranged statistical facts. This is seen in the way he recorded his self imposed task, for instance he spent a total number of twenty seven days walking with an additional two on travel. The total time was two hundred and seven hours (which included halts for note taking, eating and bathing). The distance covered was three hundred and ninety six miles at an average of two and a quarter miles per hour and the height ascended was eight nine thousand three hundred feet.

The area which Donald defined as the Uplands of the Scottish Lowlands stretched from the Ochils in the North to the Galloway Hills and the Cheviots in the south (although Scotland had only half a share on two out of the seven tops in the latter). The whole layout was based on Munro's Tables but differed in one respect that the 'best ascended column', originally in the tables, was scrapped and a column for 'distinguishing summit marks, ridges, fences and dykes for assistance in misty weather' was included. Today's S.M.C. guide follows this outline but the above column was removed after the 1974 edition.

8

Donald set about defining his tops and hills using the following rules and the one inch map of the day. Tops were to be: "all elevations with a drop of 100 feet on all sides and elevations of sufficient topographical merit with a drop of 100 and 50 feet on all sides". The hills were: "groupings of 'tops' into hills, except where applicable on topographical grounds, on the basis that 'tops' are not more than 17 units from the main top of the 'hill' to which they belong." What were the units? These were defined as either a twelfth of a mile along a connecting ridge or one 50 feet contour between the lower top or col. In addition he also mentioned 15 'humps' with 2,000feet contours.

Throughout the walk whether it was Tinto, the first hill to be climbed, or on Blackcraig hill, the last, conditions were often tough with bog and mist in the cols or extremely poor visibility on the tops. Donald walked all these hills on his own with one exception, Cairnsmore of Fleet. He was almost shot at on one occasion and had frozen knees on another (he wore the kilt throughout – even mentioning its unsuitability for glissading in). There is even a word about litter on the top of Cheviot and how he enjoyed a pint, a hot bath and supper (in that order) in a hotel at Carsphairn. He records all in minute detail but he forgets to mention the wild rugged beauty of these lonely often forgotten hills.

Advice to Walkers and Access in the Donalds

All these hills offer a peace and tranquillity with panoramic views over rolling countryside. There are lochs, burns, waterfalls, wildlife and wild flowers to see and explore amongst unspoilt tracts of land where few people go. The light provides unusual effects on the land and gives the photographer or painter an excuse to stop and admire.

The walker has a choice of walking the hills described as a complete days walk or as part of a long distance expedition using the Southern Upland Way and Pennine Way. The hills may also be walked individually.

Although not as rugged as the hills of the Scottish Highlands or the Lake District they can show a wildness and remoteness of their own where there is often bog and thick heather or bracken to walk through or impassable forest to go round.

Therefore the walks should not be undertaken lightly but planned carefully giving care and safety to others. There is a need for food, strong footwear (preferably walking boots), suitable clothing, first-aid, emergency rations, bivvy bag and a whistle to be carried. A map and compass are also needed with the ability to use them in the hills where weather conditions can change very rapidly. In winter ice axe and crampons should be carried and if skiing due care should be taken.

Please do not spoil the magnificent beauty of these hills for yourself or others. Always take your litter home, do not light fires, avoid damaging property, close gates, keep dogs under control, keep to the paths if asked and generally protect and care for the countryside.

During 2004 there was new legislation introduced where there is a legal right of responsible access to most land and water in Scotland giving a better understanding of the tradition of 'freedom to roam'. Responsibilities of users and land managers are described in the Scottish Outdoor Access Code published by Scottish Natural Heritage (visit www.snh.org.uk for more information). These lands provide jobs and revenue to many people and support rural communities – please respect their wishes when it comes to lambing and access to grouse and deer moors during the shooting season. There is space for everyone.

The walker is also reminded to leave details with someone of where they are going. Remember that the mountain rescue services are voluntary bodies that carry out an excellent service. Please do not take them for granted.

The Ochils

The Ochils

O.S. MAP: Landranger Series 58
                    Perth to Alloa

DONALDS: (in order walked)

NAME	HEIGHT	MAP REF
Innerdownie	611m/2004ft	966031
Tarmangie Hill	645m/2117ft	942014
King's Seat Hill	648m/2125ft	936998
Ben Cleuch	721m/2363ft	903006
Blairdenon Hill	631m/2073ft	866018

SUGGESTED STARTING POINT: NS 964984

COMPLETE ROUND: 32km/20miles

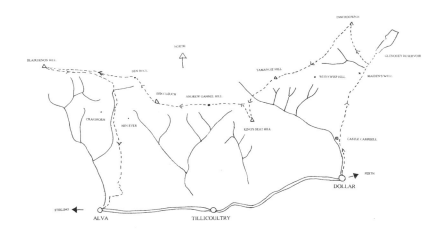

SIGHTS OF INTEREST: A historic area with Castle Campbell (at one time the principal Lowland seat of the Argyll family) the Mill trail and Dollar itself to visit. In 1715 the Battle of Sheriffmuir took place to the north west of Blairdenon Hill.

NOTES: These are a range of hills in Central Scotland which extend from Auchertermuchty to Bridge of Allan in an east, north-east direction. The summits are highest at the south west end.

The walk described requires transport back to the starting point. There is a good bus service along this route (A91) or a bike may be used. The starting point can of course be at either end. If wished each hill can be walked separately or as two rounds where the end and starting point would be the same.

ROUTE : Park in Dollar and walk beside the Burn of Sorrow through the town, following the signs to Castle Campbell. As you near Castle Campbell the path wanders through a rocky glen of deciduous wood and rushing water. If time permits enter the castle as it is worth a visit. Otherwise walk along the tarred road for a short distance until you come to a white cottage and sign post indicating the Drove Road to Glendevon. Take this pleasant track where you pass the Maiden's Well, known for its magical powers, and continue to walk until the beginning of Glenquey Reservoir.

The first climb of the day starts from here over tussock grass with hidden hollows. Walk in a north westerly direction to gain the top of Innerdownie, where there is a cairn a few metres from the dyke. From here the first of the wonderful views are seen: the Devon valley and Forth lie to the south; to the north lie the Grampians, Ben Vorlich, Stuc a Chroin and more on a clear day. Closer the reservoirs of Glenquey, Glensherup and Glendevon can be seen. Just below the top is the remains of a shelter useful in adverse conditions.

Follow the faint line of a path south west beside the dyke and forestry fence, guarding a well established forest. There are also signs of new planting gradually encroaching further and further up the hillside. Progress is good at this stage. Whitewisp Hill, a top, is slightly off route but can be easily taken in as you pass on your way.

Tarmangie Hill or the 'Hill of the Goats' lies slightly off the fence line on a hummock with a small cairn. It too gives a good impression of the surrounding countryside and the route ahead. Continue south westwards for about 100 metres or so until the fence travels off towards Maddy Moss in a westerly direction. Leave the Region Boundary fence at this point and descend steeply down to the Burn of Sorrow where a pleasant, fairly sheltered spot gives a good excuse for a breather before the steep climb southwards over long tussock grass to King's Seat Hill.

This hill, about halfway, is the second highest of the round. On it is a reasonable cairn and a small dyke shelter which, when the wind blows is most welcome. From here stock can be taken of the distance gained, for not far below stands the profile of Castle Campbell, in the distance is Innerdownie and in front Ben Cleuch. If the prospect daunts then a return via Bank Hill or a direct descent down to the Burn of Sorrow can be taken back to the starting point.

A different direction is now taken for Andrew Gannel Hill. This is not a Donald but a top and in order to continue must be climbed. Strike north west and then descend again steeply to Gannel Burn and another drove road, this time through to Blackford in Strathallan from Mill Glen above Tillicoultry. These routes emphasise how important the Ochils once were to the traveller - a division between the Highlands and the richer Lowland plains.

Tussock grass is found at low level but is soon left behind as you stride over the tops towards Ben Cleuch, highest of the day. A view point pillar, large cairn and dyked shelter, indicate the top and the popularity of the hill. It is also where the easy walking stops and bog takes over. Again, if wished, there is a way off by going over The Law and then down the Mill Glen to Tillicoultry.

From here walk to the lesser heights of Blairdenon Hill by way of Ben Buck, drop steeply down to the col where the going suddenly becomes less enjoyable for there is a light green moss which can become wet as a sponge after heavy rain and peat hag equally distasteful. There is however a way round even though more time consuming, a fence goes to Blairdenon and in this case will take you to the top. However, always use a fence with extreme caution and watch this area in mist. The top of Blairdenon Hill is the meeting point of three fences and is 110m lower than Ben Cleuch so less dramatic but on a fine day worth going out to as the views from here are marvellous.

For the descent to Alva take a south east bearing over the moss and bog to a good track between Ben Ever and Craighorn which takes you down to a road.

VERDICT: This is a long but enjoyable walk with impressive views over the Lowlands and towards the Highlands. In places it can give tricky navigation especially in mist and there is some marshy ground in places but definately well worth doing.

Looking from Tarmangie Hill
to Glenquey Reservoir

The Moorfoot Hills

The Moorfoot Hills.

O.S. MAP: Landranger Series 73

Peebles, Galashiels & Surrounding Area.

DONALDS: (in order walked)

NAME	HEIGHT	MAP REF
Route 1		
Jeffries Corse (Dundreich)	622m/2040ft	275491
Bowbeat Hill	626m/2050ft	292469
Blackhope Scar	651m/2137ft	315483
Route 2.		
Whitehope Law	620m/2038ft	330446
Windlestraw Law	659m/2163ft	372431

SUGGESTED STARTING POINT: Route 1 NT 293527   Route 2 NT 339434

COMPLETE ROUND: Route 1 - 16km/10miles.   Route 2 - 12km/7½ miles.

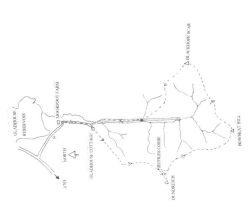
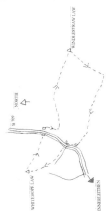

SIGHTS OF INTEREST:

Route 1: Gladhouse Reservoir built to supply Edinburgh with water and Hirendean Castle with its unrecorded past.

Route 2: The small town of Innerleithen is south of this walk. On the main street is John Smail's printing works (a National Trust Property) and nearby is St. Ronan's Well. Two miles away is Traquair, the oldest inhabited house in Scotland. The whole area shows signs of ancient settlements.

NOTES: Both walks can be combined if wished but it would be helpful to have transport arranged at either end.

There is adequate accommodation to be found either at Edinburgh, Peebles or Innerleithen. Innerleithen has a small golf course.

There is grouse moorland, especially on route 2, so are best walked out of season. They provide good skiing.

ROUTE 1: These hills lie south of Gladhouse Reservoir and may be reached by taking the B6372 road from Penicuick or the unclassified road from Waterheads on the A703 Peebles/Edinburgh road. A small narrow road from here leads to Moorfoot Farm. It is not practical to park at the farm but parking places are available lower down.

The Moorfoot Hills can be seen from Moorfoot Farm and the track goes up the South Esk valley from here. Walk up the track to Gladhouse Cottage behind which is a dyke. Follow this up the lower slopes of Jeffries Corse until it joins with the Regional Boundary fence between Lothian and the Borders. Jeffries Close is named by Donald as the top and there is a small cairn here but the real summit, Dundreich, lies just south west and has an ordnance survey pillar. To reach Dundreich follow a fence on a South West bearing from Jeffries Corse to where it terminates with an old dyke, the pillar is close by.

To continue return to the Boundary fence and bear south east to Bowbeat Hill. Two options are available here depending on the weather. In clear weather walk across the tops to the col between Bowbeat Hill and Jeffries Close, in thick mist there is a fence as a guide. This fence dips down steeply to the start of the Leithen Water and the narrow upper reaches of a fairly remote glen, when you meet the forestry plantation bear east (keep the forestry fence on your right) to start the ascent for Bowbeat Hill.

Bowbeat lies at the head of the South Esk River valley and gives a good view out across the reservoir on a clear day. This part of the walk is boggy with many peat hags so as a consequence takes longer to traverse than the 2½km imply. Emily Bank, a mere pimple, comes next and here the forestry reappears by the side of the fence. An alternative route to these hills is by the forestry track from Leithen Lodge which emerges here. By using this route it would be possible to combine Whitehope Law in the same day .

Blackhope Scar lies on a north easterly bearing from here and gives a walk of 3km over more peat hag but here at least it is a little less boggy than the previous section. Blackhope Scar is the highest of the three and also has an ordance survey pillar, found at a meeting of three fences. Just before the top is reached a further fence coming from Rough Moss is seen. This is a district fence and would be followed for a while if Whitehope was going to be traversed. A warning though - the name Garvald Punks, which would have to be walked to from Blackhope Scar, lives up to its name.

On a good day the walk can be extended from Blackhope Scar along the Moorfoots to Mauldslie Hill or further. The other way off, especially in mist, is to follow the Long Cleave burn down to the South Esk valley then take the landrover track to Moorfoot Farm, passing on the way the remains of Hirendean Castle standing above the track and east of Gladhouse Cottage.

VERDICT: The walk is longer than the map distance would suggest as the conditions underfoot are not ideal but it gives a pleasant day with good views.

ROUTE 2: To arrive at the start for this day take the B709 from the centre of Innerleithen. This road goes through the golf course along the Leithen Valley until it passes into the Glentress Valley. Shortly on the east side of the road is seen Glentress Cottage and nearby there is space for parking.

Climb Whitehope Law first by crossing the Glentress Water, easily fordable in normal conditions, and walk up the small burn between Windside Hill and an old plantation of pine trees. There is just over 320 metres of ascent at this point and the top is soon reached. A fence passes along the top and beside a thicker fence post is a very small summit cairn. The top gives an excellent view of the Glensax Hills and the other Moorfoots. The going is reasonable with grass on the lower slopes and heather on the upper.

Now take a south easterly bearing for Blackhopebyre and descend down a steep slope to this modernised cottage, recross the stream and road to start the walk up to Windlestraw Law. There is space here for cars to park if wished. A green road, not marked on the map, leaves from this point and is followed up onto Glentress Rig. The going again is easy and time can be taken to enjoy the unfolding views.

The path fades on the grouse moor at the shooting butts so a walk over rough ankle high heather begins and then terminates at a fence which has come up from Blackhopebyre Burn. The heather becomes shorter and gives way to moss, cloudberry and blaeberry with the odd patch of peat hag. Walk alongside this fence eastwards until it joins the district fence on the top of Windlestraw Law. The ordance

18

survey pillar is just north of the junction of the fences and is easily seen in all but the thickest of mists.

A subsidiary ridge runs south-east from the top to Glede Knowe and gives an easy walk to another excellent viewpoint from where the Leithen Water valley and Tweed valley can both be seen with a panorama of the Minch and Glensax Hills over to Dollar Law.

Once this point is reached the return to the start is by the spot height 654 and thence to Bareback Knowe north-west of here. A slightly steep descent down to Glentress burn and a walk back beside it brings you back to Glentress cottage and the end of the walk.

VERDICT: This is a medium length walk but there is a steep descent and so height is lost between the two hills which has to be regained. Whitehope Law can be attached to the first route and Windlestraw Law can be climbed from the A72 either from Innerleithen or Walkerburn.

The broad summit of Windlestraw

Tinto Hill

Tinto Hills.

O.S. MAP: Landranger Series 72
                 Upper Clyde Valley.

DONALD

NAME	HEIGHT	MAP REF.
Tinto	707m /2,335ft	953344

SUGGESTED STARTING POINT: NS 954323

COMPLETE WALK : 8km/5mls

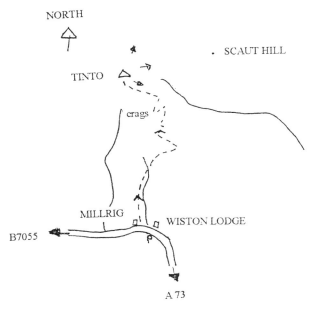

TOTHERIN HILL

NORTH

SCAUT HILL

TINTO

crags

MILLRIG

WISTON LODGE

B7055

A 73

SITES OF INTEREST: Nearby is the pleasant town of Biggar with a museum and "The Purvis Puppet" theatre.

NOTES: The name Tinto signifies 'Hill of Fire' or red and is said to have connections with Druidical rites once performed on its summit. It is suggested there were Iron age connections with this hill and around the lower slopes are evidence of forts. There has always been an immense cairn at the summit and it is alleged to have grown by the carrying of stones in way of a penance from a church situated in a small glen north east of the hill (possibly at Thankerton?). Over the years many beacon fires have been set alight on its top one in particular is remembered for the King's Jubilee in May 1935.

The view indicator on Tinto was first erected on 13th September 1935. It is a masonary pillar 1m high with a circular disc of Doulton stoneware, a useful map outline of the neighbouring country was placed in the centre of the design.

Tinto hill is a prominent landmark so it is not surprising that many popular rhymes and poems have been written about it.

To quote one: "Tinto Top
                    between
                    Culter Fell
                    is of an ell."

(an ell was a measure of a yard and a quarter or 1.2m)

ROUTE: Tinto Hill is found in the Clydesdale District, to the east of the river Clyde and to the west of the Douglas Water. It is difficult to combine this hill with any other Donald. A short day can be made of it or perhaps the walk can be continued up one path and then down another side of the hill. This may pose a problem as all descents end on the main A73, a very busy road.

The short route up this superb little hill is from Millrig Farm on the B7055. Parking is available near Wiston Lodge, a Y.M.C.A. hostel for national training. Walk a few metres along the road to the farm and a gate which opens onto a track leading across a grass field to a fence. Follow the fence till a zig-zag path is seen going round the grey stone of Pap Craig. These crags look impressive either on the map or in reality and care should be taken in mist. The path allows an easy approach up an otherwise steep ascent.

The heather and blaeberry slopes disappear and the red sandstone which dominates the top stands out. The path reunites with the fence and the top is soon gained. The cairn is encircled by a fence and fences can be seen radiating out from the top pointing the way to other possibilities of descent or ascent. Views of Culter Fell, Gathersnow and Pykestone Law are seen and if not too hazy the far away hills of Ben Vorlich and

Ben Lomond.

The long way back is by Totherin Hill, it has a rather large cairn, then to Fallburn. Those in more of a hurry or with transport problems can descend by way of Scaut Hill to Broadlees or return by their ascent route. Whichever decision is arrived at, it is certainly worth while on a sunny day to spend time on the top admiring the views .

VERDICT: Although a shorter day than many of the other walks described in this book, it is a tremendous hill with great views from the summit.

Tinto, 'The Hill of Fire'

The Culter Hills

THE CULTER HILLS

O.S.MAP :   Landranger Series 72.

Upper Clyde Valley.

DONALDS.

NAME	HEIGHT	MAP REF.
Hudderstone	626m(2055ft)	022272
(formerly Heatherstone)		
Hillshaw Head	653m(2141ft)	048246
Gathersnow Hill	689m(2262ft)	059257
Culter Fell	748m(2454ft)	053291
Chapelgill Hill	696m(2382ft)	068304

SUGGESTED STARTING POINT: NT 035305 or NT 035284

COMPLETE ROUND: 23km/14miles

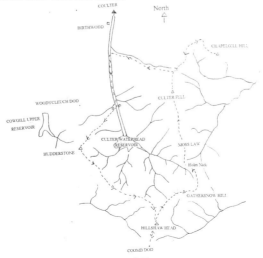

SIGHTS OF INTEREST: There are pre-historic remains and several forts to be found in the lower part of the valley, just south of Coulter.

NOTE: These hills form the highest part of hill country between the Clyde and the Upper Tweed. Each hill can be walked individually or as a combination with others. Red grouse are plentiful so access between August and December is not encouraged (the walker as elsewhere must share the hills with other sports).

ROUTE: Travel on the A702 to the small village of Coulter (about 10km. from Biggar) then take the narrow road to Birthwood. The road at this point splits into two, so take the left or east branch leading to Culter Waterhead Reservoir. Half a kilometre on this road, where the Kings Beck burn joins Culter Water, it is possible to park. The day can start from here by ascending Chapelgill Hill first and ending on Hudderstone if wished.

Alternatively go further up the road until a farm shed is seen by Lea Gill. This small stream drains off Hudderstone and the neighbouring hills into the Culter Water. Follow Lea Gill steeply up over heather, rough grass and moss to the col between Hudderstone and Woody Cleuch Dod. Bear south to a top which levels out. A small cairn marks the summit and from here a fence is seen coming from Ward Law, this continues to Dod Hill.

Glimpses of Cowgill Reservoir, Culter Reservoir and beyond can be seen as you walk beside the fence to Dod Hill and The Bank. Here an unmarked right of way passes across from Culter Reservoir down to Wandel on the A702, a good walk if the forestry can be avoided. Ground conditions between Hudderstone and The Bank are distinctly squelchy in places and damp in others.

The mist can move in quickly over these hills, but on a clear day forest, water and the rolling countryside can be seen. The fence continues, branches and then joins the Region Boundary between the Borders and Strathclyde to Hillshaw Head top, a small cairn with an iron fence post sticking out marks the spot, slightly to the east of the fence.

Coomb Dod, no longer a Donald, lies south of Hillshaw Head and is only a short distance out of the way. It is well worth the effort for the view from the ordnance survey pillar stretches out to the east beyond Broad Law and south to Hart Fell.

Gathersnow Hill is north of Hillshaw Head and lies at the head of the reservoir. If Coomb Dod is visited then retrace your footsteps to Hillshaw Head and continue along the District fence. As you walk the outline of Broad Law, one of the Border Corbetts as well as a Donald, looms up to the east and views continue to be good over to Culter Fell. The going becomes easier and after a small incline Gathersnow is soon reached (as the name suggests Gathersnow does tend to hold the snow in winter).
From here it is a short distance to Glenwhappen Rig and a steep descent down to Holm Nick, where the Culter Water rises. The Culter then passes into Culter Waterhead Reservoir and drains eventually into the Clyde. Its origins lie in an impressive cleft which formed a refuge in the 1745 rebellion from the army of Highlanders which

passed by. They were returning North and on the look out for any cattle to take back to their crofts. The laird at the time, a Mr Gladstone, organised all the cattle in the area to be removed up to Holm Nick. Today it provides good shelter for sheep or for walkers.

A track from this spot leads down to the house at the end of the reservoir and offers a possible way off if desired. Ahead is a steep climb up to Moss Law and Culter Fell. This hill has character and gives a good view point over to the Manor Hills and beyond. Progress up Moss Law can be slow with excuses to stop and catch glimpses of Holms Water Glen, almost Highland in appearance were it not for more signs of habitation.

The ordnance survey pillar on Culter Fell soon appears. It is the highest point of the whole round, falling short of being a Corbett by only 14 metres, and is a popular hill for walkers. This hill can also be ascended from Holm Water or over Cardon Hill from Kilbucho. The fence continues along the tops following King Bank Head and over Scawdmans Hill to eventually terminate at the West Lothian District boundary in the Pentlands.

To gain the last Donald walk along the fence to King Bank Head and then toward Cardon Hill. When the fence turns sharp north west towards Scawdmans Hill take a south east bearing. This can be an extremely difficult move in mist and although there is a fence off at this point it leads down to forestry and Holm Water valley. Southwards is a steeply contoured descent to Hope Burn. The terrain is rough being mainly over peat hag and heather tussocks. The top is marked by a small summit cairn and gives further views over to Drumelzier Law, Pykestone and Dollar Law.

Return by King Bank Head then westwards to Tippet Knowe. The descent down to Kings Beck is steep over heather with some loose rock but at the foot there is a Landrover track to follow. This takes you back to the road near Birthwood either to transport or a 1.5km walk along the road to Lea Gill and the shed.

VERDICT: This walk offers a pleasant walk in a beautiful area of the Borders and gives even the fittest a strenuous day.

Culterfell Round on
a winter day

The Manor Hills

The Manor Hills

Route 1.

O.S. MAP: Landranger Series No.72 /73

Upper Clyde Valley /Peebles, Galashiels & Surrounding Area.

DONALDS: (arranged in order walked)

NAME:	HEIGHT	MAP REF.
Talla Cleuch Head	690m(2264ft)	134218
(Muckle Side)		
Broad Law	840m(2754ft)	146235
Cramalt Craig	30m(2723ft)	169248
Dollar Law	817m(2680ft)	178278
Greenside Law	643m(2110ft)	198256
Black Law	697m(2285ft)	224280

SUGGESTED STARTING POINTS: NT 151203 or NT 195229

COMPLETE ROUND: 34km/21 miles

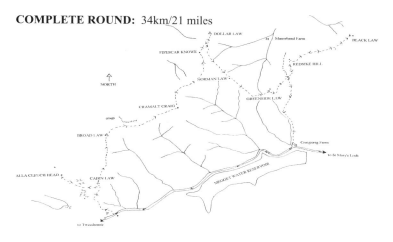

SIGHTS OF INTEREST: Close by is St.Mary's Loch, a natural loch of great beauty with the famous 'Tibby Shields' Inn meeting house of James Hogg (The Ettrick Shepherd) and his friend Sir Walter Scot.

Not far from Craigierig is the small hamlet of Glengaber which was entered on the Crown Roll as early as 1455. Gold was discovered here by the Regent Morton in the 16th. century but the amount must have been small as nothing came of it. Nearby in the heart of the whole valley is Henderland, the home of the Cockburn family. It is thought that they were the hereditary standard bearers to Irmin the Saxon Warlord who invaded Lothian during the 6th.century. Below this round of hills is the Megget Water a reservoir opened in 1983.

The area was once the favourite hunting grounds of the Kings of Scotland. The hunting lodge tower was at Cramalt, where now a farmhouse stands backed by firs and birches. The tower, or what remains of it, is hidden in sheep folds but Bishop Lesley in the 16th. century said this area "Gave harbourage to the largest stags in Scotland". Both James IV and V hunted here and even Mary Queen of Scots brought Darnley here to hunt. Between Cramalt and Craigierig on the hill named Hunter Hill or in those days Green Hill lies a great quantity of rocks and boulders, one of which looks like a huge chair. This is known as the 'Queen's Chair' from which Queen Mary or possibly Margaret Tudor is supposed to have watched tilting, mentioned in James Hoggs tale of "The Bride of Polmood". The most common way for the hunting parties to arrive was by the Thieves Road.

NOTES: Broad Law is also a Corbett.

Most of these hills can be done as individual hills or in smaller groups if desired.

The picnic areas around the Megget Water are well designed and have information boards describing how the dam and reservoir were constructed.

The main features are the high ridges running northwards from the Megget watershed along the west side of the Manor Water with a lower ridge running north east to divide and form the valley of Glensax.

ROUTE: The starting point is the Megget Stone, but to give less of a walk at the end of the day the car may be left at the picnic site found beside the Megget Reservoir, west of the Cramalt Burn. It is a peaceful spot enjoyed by fishermen, walkers and holidaymakers.

To reach the Megget Stone, a distance of about 3km from the starting point, means a pleasant walk along a minor road which connects Tweedsmuir to St.Mary's Loch. The road keeps beside the reservoir to Meggethead and then branches to the right to connect the Megget Water with the Talla Reservoir, above which the first Donald of the walk, Talla Cleuch Head, is to be found.

The Megget Stone, some say the possible site of King Arthur's last battle, is at the highest point on this road and sits on the District Boundary. Follow the boundary fence from the Megget Stone north to Fans Law and then towards Cairn Law where the fence angles off to the right bear north west and left to another fence coming from Talla Cleuch Head. Walk with care round the crags and look below on a clear day to see Talla Linfoots farm. The sides continue to be steep as you climb the aptly named Muckle Side to Talla Cleuch Head, unnamed on the 1:50,000 map (reference point 134218). When you arrive there is no obvious top, cairn or even thicker fence post to indicate the summit. However, it is worth the detour as it is a good view point with the Culter Hills dominating to the west, while south lie White Coomb and the hills surrounding the Grey Mare's Tail. (This walk can be continued to Mathieside and then steeply down to Talla Reservoir if a return to Cairn Law is not desired).

To walk to Cairn Law reverse your bearings to pick up the boundary fence. Walk beside this passing a large number of cairns on your way to the top. With a north bearing continue to follow the fence for 3km along the wide ridge to Broad Law, the walking is easy and progress fast over the short grass and lichen. Not much has changed in these hills since February 1891 when the members of the newly formed Scottish Mountaineering Club climbed Broad Law on their first club meet except the summit, for as you approach a flying saucer shaped radio beacon and two tall radio masts draw the eye away from the ordnance survey pillar which acts as the cairn.

Vehicles are used to service these masts so the top is scarred by tracks and wheel marks which rather detracts from this pleasant hill. The track comes up from Hearthstane and would allow an easy walk to the top from the north west if wished. The walk continues on a north east bearing over to Cramalt Craig, once a Corbett but now deleted. From this point look down to Megget Water and across to the hills beyond, if the weather permits, for the blue of the water contrasts with the green and purple of the hills and gives ideal light for photography.

The route now changes from an easterly bearing to a more northerly one for Dollar Law but there is a dry stone wall to follow as well as a fence to Fifescar Knowe which lies on the way. From here, along the contours below Dollar Law, can be seen the bright green of the Thieves Road. This track goes through the Borders to Mid-Lothian and was the path taken by the moss troopers, it is no longer distinct in places although seen perfectly from here. Pykestone Hill, Drumelzier Law and Middle Hill stand out against the skyline.

The next two hills are lower, but in relation to Dollar Law quite a distance away. As usual, review the situation to see if it is worth going on or return by the Thieves road to the starting point. If the decision is reached to continue then a return to Norman Law is required. From this top there is a steep descent and then a swing round the Manor Water valley, Manorhead farm can be seen at the bottom of Dollar Law.

Greenside Law is fairly nondescript but lives up to its name as the slope you ascend is

31

very green in comparison to the surrounding hills. The top is north west of the fence and has no obvious cairn or fence post to indicate a summit (remember to replace map 72 with map 73 here). Another descent to the valley and the track between Megget Water and Manor Water brings you to a gate in the fence with an obvious track going north/south. Nearby there is a small sheep shelter (useful also for humans if the weather turns bad).

Follow the fence over Redsike Hill to Black Law (on the map the actual Donald is the spot height of 696m slightly north east of Black Law). This part of the walk is indescribably boggy but once up walking is slightly easier and there is a new fence to follow. This area is mainly used for grouse shooting so during August to December should be avoided. The Donald top has three fences coming together but no cairn and from here the Dun Rig round of Donalds can be seen with views over the lesser heights to the south. It is possible to continue on but transport would have to be arranged at Peebles otherwise return back to the track seen earlier at the gap between Redsike and Greenside.

The return does not take long and you are soon back to the gate. Go through this and take the track back to the Craigierig farm resited after the flooding of the valley to create Megget Water. From this point the walk is little under a kilometre back to the picnic spot and the car but sometimes seems further after a long day.

VERDICT: A long walk but the ground on the whole is reasonable, especially in dry conditions, but tackle all the walk only if fit and experienced. Many shorter but still enjoyable days can still be had in this area.

Looking towards Dollar Law from Broom Hill, Peebles

The Manor Hills

Route 2.

O.S. MAP: Landranger Series No.72 /73

Upper Clyde Valley /Peebles, Galashiels & Surrounding Area.

DONALDS: (arranged in order walked)

NAME:	HEIGHT	MAP REF.
Pykestone Hill	737m/24114ft	173313
Middle Hill	715m/2340ft	159294
Drumelzier Law	668m/2191ft	149313

SUGGESTED STARTING POINT: NT135342

COMPLETE ROUND: 16km/10 mls.

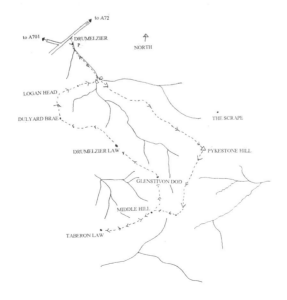

SIGHTS OF INTEREST: Nearby is Dawyck House gifted to the nation to become part of the Royal Botanic Garden, Edinburgh in 1979. There is an important collection of mature trees and rhododendrons. It is open daily from spring to Autum.

The area is also famous for its castles; one of which is Drumelzier Castle once used as a sentinel tower to guard the Upper Tweed valley. This was the property of the powerful Tweedie family who gained prominence in the 16th.century but after 1670 seemed to disappear from Scottish history.

It is also said where the Drumelzier or Powsail Burn meets the Tweed the remains of Merlin, the wizard, are to be found. One of Thomas the Rhymers famous prophesies was:

> "When Tweed and Powsail meet at Merlin's grave,
>
> Scotland and England shall one monarch have."

Tradition states on the very day James VI was crowned King of England the Tweed over flowed and joined the Powsail Burn.

ROUTE: Take the road to Drumelzier on the B712 (off the A701) - there is adequate parking available at the village. The walk starts from this point beside the Drumelzier or Powsail Burn and goes through two small plantations with buildings nearby. Continue on this track to Den Knowes and take the right track, the left goes to The Scrape. Keep on the track and bear slightly to the south east until you hit the fence. Follow this and the ordance survey pillar on Pykestone's summit is soon reached.

From the top of Pykestone a south west bearing is taken which in fact follows the fence to Long Grain Knowe by the Thief's Road and would lead on to Dollar Law. On Long Grain Knowe is a three way fence, when this is reached take a bearing west for Middle Hill (there is an old fence to follow but it is usually better to work on compass bearings).

Middle Hill has no cairn or fence post to mark the summit but once land descends all round you know the top is reached. From this point it is an easy stroll over to Taberon Law (now a deleted Donald but a good view point). However you must retrace your footsteps to Middle Hill to continue and walk back to the 700m contour line, almost to the gentle col between Middle Hill and Long Grain Knowe. A northerly bearing will take you to Glenstivon Dod where there is a well built medium sized cairn and a good view point of Pykestone Hill, Drumelzier Law, Middle Hill and further.

Between Glenstivon Dod and Drumelzier Hill is a steep descent and an equally steep climb but it is soon over and the last Donald of the day reached. From here you can either drop down to the path and so back or preferably walk along the ridge to

Dulyard Brae, Logan Head and Finlen Rig to take in the views of the Culter Fell Round and the valleys in between. When Finglen Rig is reached descend back to the track at the farm steading and follow the track back to the starting point.

VERDICT: An enjoyable walk over heather moor but in mist these hills provide a challenge and so a good knowledge of a map and compass is required. In winter these hills can provide good cross country skiing.

A winter's day over Pykestone and Drumelzier

Route 3.

O.S. MAP: Landranger Series No.72 /73

Upper Clyde Valley /Peebles, Galashiels & Surrounding Area.

DONALDS: (arranged in order walked)

NAME:	HEIGHT	MAP REF.
Birkscairn Hill	662m/2169ft	275332
Dun Rig	742m/2433ft	253316
Glenrath Heights	730m/2382ft	241323
Stob Law	676m/2218ft	230333

SUGGESTED STARTING POINT: NT 260392

COMPLETE ROUND: 22km/14 miles.

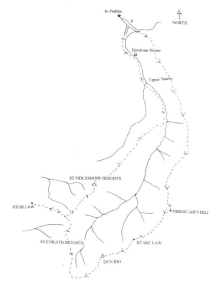

SIGHTS OF INTEREST: Peebles is a historic town and worth a visit. During the month of June the town comes alive to the Beltane Festival where there is a carnival atmosphere. There is also the Chamber's Museum to visit.

NOTES: In 1977 an abortive attempt was made to light a beacon from Dun Rig for Queen Elizabeth's Silver Jubilee Celebrations.

ROUTE: These hills surround the Glensax Valley and form a pleasant walk. To reach them go to Peebles and follow the Kings Muir road until it terminates at the Haystoun House private road. Walk down the grass lane straight ahead which soon narrows to cross a burn by a footbridge beside Whitehaugh Farm. This glen is known as the Gypsy or Fairy Glen. The path climbs through pleasant woodland up onto an old drove road which brought cattle down from the north and goes across to St Mary's Loch. Two dykes on either side of the path show how wide the road once was and you can almost hear the talk of the drovers and the noise of the cattle as they passed by. From here great views down to Peebles can be seen and once on Birkscairn Hill views across Cardona Forest open up.

Ahead and slightly to the south west at the top of the glen is Dun Rig, below is the Glensax Valley and to the west Hundleshope Heights. Descend to the col between Birkscairn and Stake Law, here the drove road leaves to head between the two Stake Laws and go over to St Mary's Loch. Keep to the high ground and head for the higher Stake Law, the going between this hill and Dun Rig can be boggy at times and shows some signs of erosion. It does not take long though until the ordance survey pillar of Dun Rig is reached and the views continue to impress as from here all the Manor Hills can be seen. It is possible to walk all the way to the Megget Stone and further from this point if wished.

Continue the walk, cross a flat plateau for about a kilometre or so and then turn sharply right to go west and follow the fence to Glenrath Heights. The views across the Forth and Pentlands to Arthur's Seat and Largo Law are superb. Over to the east lie the Moorfoots and to the far north Ben More and Stob Binnein can be seen, south are the Cheviots and the Eildons.

At Broomhill north of Glenrath Heights a diversion is required to take in Stob Law, the last of the four Donalds on this round. Follow the fence steeply down to the col and then straight up again to a very small cairn which lies just north of the fence and here if anything the panoramas are better. Below at Glenrath is Macbeth's Castle (no connection to Macbeth in Shakesphere's play). The hill here falls steeply northwards down to Hundleshope Burn giving an impression of height. A return to Broom Hill brings you back onto the main route to Hundleshope Heights where there is another ordance survey pillar and where you descend down the right hand spur to the Glensax

37

Valley. Follow the landrover track past Upper Newby to Haystoun House and an 'honesty-box'. Keep to the right hand track and the tarred road which brings you back to the starting point.

VERDICT: An excellent walk over short grass and heather. Best walked before the shooting season as it is on grouse moor.

Dunrig in Glensax

The Moffat Hills

The Moffat Hills

Route 1.

O.S. MAP: Landranger Series No.72, 78/79

Upper Clyde Valley, Nithsdale & Annandale/Hawick & Eskdale area

DONALDS: (arranged in order walked)

NAME:	HEIGHT	MAP REF.
Molls Cleuch Dod	784m/2571ft	152180
Lochcraig Head	800m/2625ft	167176
White Coomb	821m/2695ft	163151
Cape Law	721m/2364ft	131151
Garelet Dod	698m/2231ft	125173
Erie Hill	688m/2259ft	124188

SUGGESTED STARTING POINT: NT 135202

COMPLETE ROUND : 24km /15 miles

SIGHTS OF INTEREST: The Grey Mare's Tail, a National Trust Property, is found south east of White Coomb and is one of the highest waterfalls in Britain, falling some 60m from the edge of the hanging valley. The vegetation is lush and there is a diversity of wildlife in the form of feral goats, ravens, gulls and sometimes eagles. Loch Skeen found above the waterfall and below Lochcraig Head is also part of the NTS.

Moffat itself is of interest and in the 1800's was a fashionable spa resort. It has hotels and a small museum.

NOTES: The Moffat Hills are the first hills of Scotland encountered by travellers from Carlisle, Hart Fell being instantly recognized.

A walk takes place every June between Peebles over the Manor Hills to the Megget Stone and then over White Coomb to Hart Fell the distance being about 64km/40 miles.

These hills are steep with deep-set valleys on the Moffat side, on the Talla Reservoir side they are slightly less sheer but tops are flat and offer excellent walking conditions mainly on grass.

There is rock climbing round Hart Fell.

If transport can be arranged it is possible to combine all these hills in a complete round but the day is extremely strenuous and long so should only be undertaken if weather conditions are good and by experienced walkers.

Recently an ancient bow was found in Rotten Bottom, it can now be found in the Scottish Museum in Edinburgh.

ROUTE: To reach the starting point for this walk take the road between the A 701 and the A 708 which connects the Megget Water and Talla Reservoir. Just south of Talla Linfoots farm, where the Games Hope Burn comes down to the Reservoir, gives a convenient start for the day. A track can be followed to Gameshope, now a ruin, with a new shed nearby. Take an easterly bearing from here for the col between Carlavin Hill and Molls Cleuch Dod. The climb is steep up short grass which then levels out to give a fine ridge walk to Molls Cleuch Dod (note that a map change is required just before the summit). Pause here to take in the wide expanse of hills: Dollar Law and the Manor Hills, to the south the higher Moffat Hills and closer Erie Hill, Garelet Dod and Cape Law. The ridge walk continues to Firthybrig Head and a good view over to Lochcraig Head, an outlier when walked from this angle.

To get to Lochcraig Head means a descent to a cleft and the col of Talla Water with a climb up to the summit on the other side. A small cairn perched on the edge of sheer cliffs which fall down to Loch Skeen proclaims the top. White Coomb is directly

41

opposite and appears close but steps must be retraced to Firthybrig Head before this hill can be reached (a return down Donald's Cleuch following the burn back to Games Hope Burn can be made if wished at this stage or descend north from Lochcraig Head by Talla East Side and Nickies Knowe).

If continuing, walk round the crags of Donald's Cleuch Head to White Coomb this lies to the south east away from the main line of the walk. It is a gentle stroll in good weather to the small summit cairn but there is little shelter from the elements to be had on a bad day. White Coomb gives the best perspective of the crags below Lochcraig Head and views of all the surrounding hills. (This hill is also a Corbett so is more frequently visited than some of the other hills.)

From here, if wished, Carrifran Gans can be visited but it does add extra distance onto an already reasonable day, it too was once a Donald. Otherwise retrace steps to the junction of the Region fence at Firthhope Rig where a map change is required from map 79 to 78.

The Region fence is followed and takes you over the boggiest part of the walk - Rotten Bottom - with the crags of Raven Craig found southwards. This bog is wet even in the driest of seasons and should be treated with great care. As you walk, the crags of Hart Fell and the sheer beauty of Saddle Yoke cheer flagging spirits and the junction for Cape Law is soon reached. Ignore the fence going up Hart Fell to the west and continue north west following a fence and dyke till a larger post than the rest is arrived at. This is the summit of Cape Law. Northwards lie a further two Donalds, Garelet Dod and Erie Hill, and the way back .

The dyke and fence continue on the same bearing and the walk is pleasant over short grass passing over Din Law to a spot height of 611m. A pull up a slight incline takes you to a fence which goes off at a 90° angle to the dyke. To take in the actual summit of Garelet Dod you must now make a north west bearing and walk for about five minutes on this from this junction, the summit point is a small hillock slightly higher than the surrounding land.

Return to the dyke which can be followed almost to the last Donald of the day, Erie Hill perched above the ruin of Gameshope. The walk from Garelet Dod is up a gentle incline and does not take long (the small summit cairn is just off the fence by an old metal post). The views are of Fruid Reservoir and across to Dollar Law. From here you can descend anywhere but crossing the burn is not easy so it is probably worth the effort to cut back to Gameshope and cross by the bridge here (there is also a bridge further down).

Now return by the track to the start.

VERDICT: This is a long day but gives a pleasant walk. However Rotten Bottom as its name suggests is very boggy and could be tricky to cross. Worth bearing in mind is the weather as this area can be difficult to negotiate in mist, there are also awkward rocky outcrops and many peat hags on this round.

White Coomb from Donald's Cleuch Head

Route 2.

O.S. MAP: Landranger Series No.78/79

Nithsdale & Annandale/Hawick & Eskdale area.

DONALDS: (arranged in order walked)

NAME:	HEIGHT	MAP REF.
Under Saddle Yoke	745m/2445ft	143126
Hart Fell	808m/2651ft	114136
Whitehope Heights	636m/2090ft	095139
Swatte Fell	730/2390ft	118114

SUGGESTED STARTING POINT: NT 1440097

COMPLETE ROUND : 19½ km/12miles

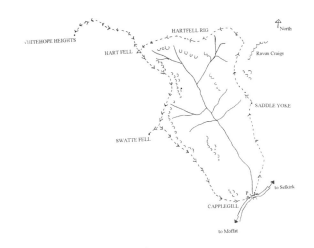

SIGHTS OF INTEREST: Same as route 1.

NOTES: Same as route 1. The descent is a very steep grassy slope.

ROUTE: The starting point for this walk is from the bridge at Cappelgill on the A708 Moffat road. The start is steep and unrelenting up the north face of Saddle Yoke but the reward of views across to the Ettrick Hills and towards Hart Fell are worth it. It is a small arete and possibly the most exciting part of the walk. Saddle Yoke is the first top reached but is not the Donald top, Under Saddle Yoke the next top is the Donald. From these tops you can gaze down at passing cars in the valley below and admire the crags opposite on Hart Fell and Swatte Fell. These are the rocks which offer the climber such scope on a fine day. A warning though, the ridge is fairly narrow and there is no fence to follow should the weather deteriorate.

From Under Saddle Yoke take a north bearing slightly west to spot height 685m on the boundary fence from Lochcraig Head to Hart Fell (it is also a Corbett). Watch out for Raven Craigs. Follow the fence on a north west bearing to Hartfell Rig which then swings south and up to the summit of Hart Fell. Although Hart Fell is lower than White Coomb it appears higher and is said to have been the home at one time of Merlin the Magician who was able to change into a hart, an animal associated with Royalty. Close by is Arthur's Seat, another possible resting place of this well known King. An ordnance survey pillar, surrounded by a small stone wall, provides shelter from any strong winds and views from here are extensive. The summit plateau is large and might be confusing in mist but the pillar is near a fence corner.

Whitehope Heights adds an extra dimension to the day as you must walk out to its top and then back to Hart Fell so involving an additional climb (if transport can be arranged at Devil's Beef Tub on the A 701 Swatte Fell should be tackled first). Follow the fence line downhill for about ten minutes to the col and then keep on a west bearing to spot height 614m, from here the bearing is south Whitehope Heights. The fence wanders off in a northerly direction so navigation to this hill can be tricky in mist.

Assuming that you have returned to Hart Fell, follow the fence southwards to Swatte Fell. The fence deviates to the east and another comes in from the west just before the summit of Swatte Fell is reached. Walk on the west fence for two hundred yards or so and the small summit cairn is soon reached.

Now return along the steep sided tops to the 723m point. From here the final descent back to the road at Cappelgill is very steep and at the end of a long day requires concentration to prevent a slip or a fall.

VERDICT: This is a superb day and the extra effort out to Whitehope Heights is worth it as you get views not seen from the other hills. If transport can be arranged for a ridge walk then the day is even better.

Be very careful, especially in mist, to avoid the crags in this area.

Looking towards Hart Fell from Coomb Fell ridge

The Ettrick Hills

The Ettrick Hills

O.S. MAP: Landranger Series 79.

Hawick and Eskdale area.

DONALDS: (arranged in order walked)

NAME	HEIGHT	MAP REF.
Ettrick Pen	692m(2270ft)	199077
Wind Fell	664m(2180ft)	179062
Loch Fell	688m(2256ft)	170047
Croft Head	636m(2085ft)	153057
Capel Fell	678m(2223ft)	164069
Bodesbeck Law	664m(2173ft)	169103
Bell Craig	623m(2046ft)	187129
Andrewhinney Hill	678m(2220ft)	198139
Herman Law	614m(2014ft)	214157

SUGGESTED STARTING POINT: NT 189092

COMPLETE ROUND: 35km/ 22 miles

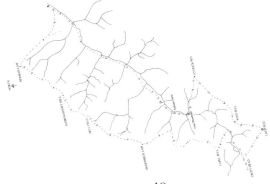

SIGHTS OF INTEREST: James Hogg monument and church at Ettrick. St Mary's Loch and Tibbie Shiel's Inn, meeting place of Sir Walter Scot and James Hogg.

NOTE: Each of these hills can be individually climbed or combined with others to make the day longer or shorter as required.

It is a good idea to have some form of transport, whether it be a second car or bike for the end of the day.

Below this round of hills lies part of the 212 mile long Southern Upland Way and at Over Phawhope is a bothy maintained by the Mountain Bothy Association.

ROUTE: Take the narrow road, which branches off the B709, from Selkirk and follow this through beautiful Border country to the small village of Ettrick. Five miles from here and about half a mile from Potburn is a locked gate. This is the base for the days walk. Walk past Potburn farm to Over Phawhope bothy where a track allows you access through the forestry, the original timber of birch and oak interspersed with ash and hazel was destroyed by James V in his efforts to convert the land into sheep pasture. Sheep are still found on the rough pasture of moor grass and heather above the conifers and during lambing walkers are not always welcomed. On the horizon is the boundary fence, still in reasonable condition, which leads to the massive pile of stones of Ettrick Pen. Below are views of Eskdalemuir and Craik Forest, both merge to form one large mass of timber interspersed with brown scars of forestry tracks. Further away is the baulk of Cheviot and the Eildons.

Follow a double boundary fence south west to a dip where two upright marker stones stand on either side of the fence then up to Hopetown Craig, a top of Ettrick Pen. From here a gentle climb leads to Wind Fell, an extra post in the boundary fence marks the top, walk out to this and then descend. South west lies Loch Fell and this time the top has an ordnance survey pillar. The descent, now north west leads down to a circular stone built sheep pen, an ideal spot for lunch. The Southern Upland long distance footpath which comes through the deep cleft between Loch Fell and Croft Head, passes this spot and provides a way back should you wish to return.

To continue the walk take the path and then start up the exposed scree of Croft Head, opposite is the scar of Craigmichan. If you enjoy scrambling, the scree is a contrast to the long grass of the previous hill. The top is marked by a junction of four fences but is worthy of more; the silver ribbon of the Solway Firth can be seen, "Galloway's' Awful Hand" spreads out behind it and four chimneys gush great white bellows of smoke, in the distant south lie the Lake District hills. Return back the same way and the outward section is now completed. This is the most distant part of the walk where hillsides are steep and in places exposed to weathered rock, so it is worthwhile taking care especially in poor conditions.

The rounded hump of Capel Fell is the next hill. The best and safest route is to walk down the path towards Potburn then follow the boundary fence, although the more direct way can be taken with care over rough scree to eventually meet the boundary fence again as you approach the top. There is no cairn to state that this is the top, instead a strainer post where the fence turns at right angles to itself to take off over grass moor marks the summit. From here to Bodesbeck Law the walk is long but now there is a well maintained dyked wall beside the fence to follow.

The hills on this side are less rounded and fall steeply down to the A708
Moffat \Selkirk road but the ridge itself offers easier walking over short grass, large patches of crowberry and heather. White Shank appears and is quickly passed on the way to the col; here a track from Potburn farm crosses to Bodesbeck and gives a way off should a shorter day be required. To continue, climb steeply northwards from the path to the rocky outcrop of Bodesbeck Law and a proper cairn. Scenically things have changed and give a good excuse for a short break. On a clear day all the Moffat hills can be seen to the west, to the east is Ettrick Pen and the hills already walked, ahead is Bell Craig to Herman Law (the last top of the day).

Bodesbeck Law to Bell Craig (watch out for severe drops and rocky outcrops on the west side) does not take long and views continue to get better: the white of the Grey Mare's Tail with Loch Skeen, normally so secretive, surrounded by the crown of rocks that is Firthybrig Head whet the appetite. The faint path in a north, north, east direction gently rises to Andrewhinney Hill, with its upright cairn then gently down to Mid Rig, Trowgrain Middle and Herman Law. At Herman Law the boundary fence\dyke goes west to Birkhill and you can continue east over Peniestone Knowe to the Southern Upland Path and follow this southwards by the Scabcleuch burn to Scabcleuch it is preferabl to take a south easterly bearing over Standtree Knowe and Cossars Hill to Cossarshill farm and rather a long road walk back to the starting point, unless transport has been arranged.

VERDICT: An excellent walk but at the end of the day it is a good idea to have transport in order to get back to the starting point. This is not a day to be undertaken lightly or in bad weather conditions even though there are fences or dykes to be followed.

The large cairn on the top of
Ettrick Pen

The Lowther Hills

The Lowther Hills

Route 1.

OS.MAPS: Landranger Series 78

Nithsdale & Annandale area.

DONALDS: (arranged in order walked)

NAME	HEIGHT	MAP REF.
Comb Law	643m/2,108ft	944075
Ballencleuch Law	691m/2,268ft	935049
Scaw'd Law	661m/2180ft	922034
Wedder Law	666m/2,186ft	938025
Gana Hill	668m/2,191ft	954011
Earncraig Hill	610m/2,000ft	973013
Queensberry	697m/2,286ft	989998

SUGGESTED STARTING POINT: NS 967072

COMPLETE WALK: 34km/20miles

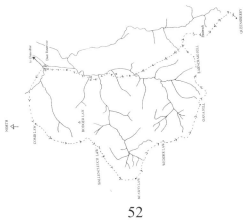

52

SIGHTS OF INTEREST: When the Daer reservoir was constructed it was possibly the largest earth dam construction in Britain. It was opened in 1956 to serve the post war population of industrial Lanarkshire. The reservoir stretches to the south west and is surrounded by a ring of high hills capped by Queensberry. Several houses lie underwater, the inhabitants being rehoused higher up on the slopes.

Both routes have the Southern Upland Way running through them.

ROUTE: Take the A702 Glasgow Dumfries road and branch off for the Daer Reservoir at Glenochar. The walk starts at the Daer Reservoir, where the Hitteril forest ends, at the bridge over Kirkhope Cleuch. Taking a westerly bearing from here, a dyke can be followed, to the top of Comb Law (there is no cairn but a fence which follows the ridge and joins the dyke - this is taken to be the summit). Pause on the top to look across to Lowther Hill in the north west with its radio masts and domes. Follow the ridge southwards to descend to a boggy col and then to Hirstane Rig. The ordnance pillar on Rodger Law (a subsidiary top of Ballencleuch) stands silhouetted against the skyline.

Fences are usually worth following when walking these hills but they never seem to go in a straight line. This one is no exception, it ducks to the west and then takes a swing to the summit of Ballencleuch where again there is no cairn. Ballencleuch can also be reached from Durisdeer.

If there is mist, walk on a south west bearing beside the fence towards Scaw'd Law to join the county boundary dyke where even in April snow can lie. The north top of Scaw'd Law is reached first and is the higher of the two. From this top a south east walk takes you to Wedder Law but first there is Carsehope Middens to cross. This is a rather boggy area and takes some careful navigation to prevent boots being sucked into the wet peat.

Once Wedder Hill has been reached descend to the col, a return to Daer Reservoir can be made from here by following the Daer Water to Kirkhope. The fence goes to Gana Hill but first there is a small hummock to go over before a descent to an area known as the Five Wells. The wells are a good feature to look for as five streams flow out of the ground to give very lush bright green grass, almost as if someone has planted it. The Five Wells lie on the lower slope of Gana Hill. Near here is the source of the River Clyde, although many other spots have also a good claim for this title. Gana Hill does have a small cairn at the east end of the hill and on a clear day gives views down the Daer Reservoir. The fence is of recent origins with signs stating that it is electric to keep the few sheep on either side separate.

From Gana's top the fence can be followed to the valley and those that want to return at this point can pick up a track further down to follow the Daer Water back to the reservoir. If continuing, it is best to take an easterly bearing for Daer Hass. Between this hillock and Earncraig Hill are a steep drop and then a steep ascent. A dyke and a fence show the way and after about ten minutes the top is gained. Earncraig Hill is far more interesting than the other hills with a rocky summit and a decent cairn. Pause and look out across the expanse of the Daer Reservoir. It is worth considering at this point whether you are fit enough to go all the way out to Queensberry and then back or whether it is better to descend down to the reservoir below.

If the decision is to continue then there are two route choices either direct or the longer route to the col following the fence, the one to be recommended in poor weather. The col connects Earncraig with Penbreck, only one metre lower and a top of Queensberry. The place to aim for from here is the Pot of Ae south east of Penbreck. At this point the fence goes off to the east and Queensberry lies sixty metres south west of this junction (the junction is marked by a strainer post). The top is round with boulders and a large cairn. William Wallace is said to have had a small skirmish with English troops on this hill and a small cairn on the south east slopes marks the spot. On a clear day the vast expanse of the Forest of Ae, owned by the Forestry Commission, can be seen stretching from north to far south of this range.

Queensberry's bold features dominate the scene and give rich views. Its name derived from the Anglo-Saxon 'berg' means hill and has somehow become 'berry'. Over many years it has given titles to the Douglas family of Earl, Marquis and Duke. The line became extinct in 1810 with the death of William the fourth Duke. The Scots family (Dukes of Buccleuch) succeeded to the Dukedom.

If wished this hill can be climbed from the south starting from Mitchellstacks farm where once James Hogg, the Ettrick Shepherd wrote an early volume of poetry. The Harkness family who were a well known Covenanting family also stayed here.

The only way back, unless transport has been arranged at this end, is a return to the col by way of Penbreck and then over the shoulder of Earncraig to the deserted cottage of Daerhead. Here a track leads down to Kirkhope at the top of the reservoir. From the top of the reservoir, where the cluster of rehoused farms and cottages are, to the start is 1.5km along a tarred road.

VERDICT: An interesting and strenuous walk with views across to the Lowther Hills but it is country where you can easily get lost especially in mist so care must be taken. It is a long day but well worth the effort as a great range of Border country is seen. Remember it is also grouse shooting country.

The summit of Lowther Hill and the radar station

Route 2.

OS.MAPS: Landranger Series 78

                          Nithsdale & Annandale area.

DONALDS: (arranged in order walked)

NAME	HEIGHT	MAP REF.
Lousie Wood Law	618m/2,028ft	932152
Dun Law	675m/2,216ft	917136
Green Lowther	732m/2,403ft	901120
Lowther Hill	725m/2,378ft	890107
East Mount Lowther	631m/2,069ft	877100

SUGGESTED STARTING POINT: NS 899152

COMPLETE WALK: 22km/14miles

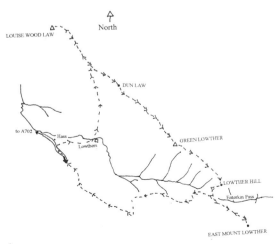

SIGHTS OF INTEREST: Both routes have the Southern Upland Way running through them. Nearby is Wanlockhead, Scotland's highest village, once a lead mining village it now has a mining museum. Gold has also been discovered in the burns at Wanlockhead. In fact James V used the gold from here for his coins and it was known as "God's Treasure House of Scotland."

It is an area of Covenanters and poets. There are tributes to the local poet Allan Ramsay (1686 - 1758) at Leadhills and gravestones to many Covenanters. Leadhills is also a mining village and another tribute is paid to William Symington "the inventor of steam navigation" who was born here.

ROUTE 2: This line of hills is found between the Mennock Water and the A 702. To reach them take the B7040 to Leadhills from Elvanfoot and park just west of Hass. Here a path which contours round the hill can be followed to Lowthers now in ruins and used by sheep for shelter.

East of Lowthers is a col between Glen Ea's Hill and Dun Law. Walk over rough heather to the fence which lies on the ridge. Leave Dun Law for later and walk on a north easterly bearing beside the fence towards Louise Wood Law. First is White Law the end of the main Lowther Ridge. Between here and Louise Wood Law is a steep cleft which must be descended with the prospect of a climb up the other side. In places slate is exposed but otherwise the walk can be slightly boggy.

Once up, there is still a fence to follow eastwards but it is joined by another two fences at the remains of a dyke. At this point it is a little over a hundred footsteps west to the summit where there is an ordnance survey pillar and a small cairn. The views from this top make up for this Donald being off the main ridge and show South Shortcleugh to the north with Tinto and Culter Fell as a further backdrop. The Daer Reservoir and its hills can be seen to the south.

A return journey must be made back to White Law by way of the steep cleft but Dun Law comes quickly and the small cairn is just east of the fence.

Between this hill and Dungrain Law there is a col but the steepest descent of the day is past. Peden Head soon follows and finally the British Telecom radio masts of Green Lowther. There is also an ordnance survey pillar here which appears insignificant by comparison but taken to be the summit. The walking conditions change considerably at this point going from rough grass, heather and moss to a tarred road.

The road leads to Lowther Hill where there is a radar station, opened just after the Second World War, and used by the Civil Aviation Authority. The rather large golf balls and radio masts stand out and form a landmark for many miles it is not generally open to the public Sadly at one time Lowther Hill was where local suicide cases were buried.

Directly below to the west is the Enterkin Pass where in 1684 an ambush took place with the rescue of six Covenanter prisoners at this point the Southern Upland Way sign posts can be seen and the path goes off towards the Daer Reservoir walk past a small shed and cross the fence to sidle over to the col and rough path for East Mount Lowther at the top is a viewpoint with a plane table erected in 1944 by the Wanlockhead Youth Club the views on a good day are superb and stretch as far as Ben More in one direction and Scafell in the other.

It is now time to return and the way off is the tarred road down to Wanlockhead, a place to visit if time permits, otherwise take the disused railway line directly back to the starting point. This line was used until 1938 connecting the Wanlockhead lead mines to Elvanfoot. Here it joined the Glasgow/Carlisle line. The track was removed but is gradually being replaced by two foot narrow gauge line laid by the local Lowther Railway Society and will eventually run between Leadhills and Wanlockhead.

VERDICT: A fairly easy day especially if Louise Wood Law is omitted. The terrain is good and stretches are even tarred. It is important to note that these hills are often in mist and in winter receive heavy falls of snow which can lie for a long time.

View from the Daer Reservoir

The Carsphairn Hills

The Carsphairn Hills

OS.MAPS: Landranger Series 77

Dalmellington to New Galloway.

DONALDS: (arranged in order walked)

NAME	HEIGHT	MAP REF.
Blackcraig Hill	700m/2298ft	648065
Blacklorg Hill	681m/2231ft	654043
Alhang	642m/2100ft	643011
Cairnsmore of Carsphairn	797m/2612ft	595980
Moorbrock Hill	651m/2136ft	621984
Windy Standard	698m/2288ft	620015

SUGGESTED STARTING POINT: NT 632065

COMPLETE WALK: 32km/20miles

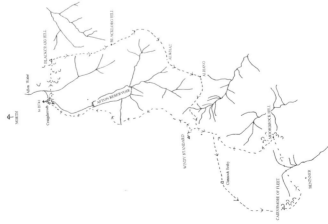

SIGHTS OF INTEREST: A memorial to Robert Burns. "There is a small river, Afton, that falls into Nith, near New Cumnock, which has some charming wild, romantic scenery on its banks." Robert Burns.

NOTES: This round provides a days walk in good weather and in the summer months there is a bothy of sorts beside the Clennoch Burn but it is very basic. The walk can be broken up into a series of smaller walks if wished and walked from different glens.

If transport can be arranged at either end i.e. Glen Afton and at Carsphairn on the A713 then the day provides a superb through walk.

ROUTE: Take the A 76 to New Cumnock and make as if to turn off for the B741 to Dalmellington but instead veer to your left immediately and follow the signs for Robert Burn's monument. This is a single track road up the beautiful Glen Afton to Afton Reservoir.

Park your vehicle opposite the cottages, just up from Craigdarroch, and walk down the track to the bridge to take you across the Afton Water. Blackcraig Hill lies directly in front and rises steeply, although rocky in places the rocks can easily be avoided and height is soon gained. In wet weather the hillside suddenly becomes alive with the gurgle of water as springs appear under your feet but they are not intimidating and can easily be circumnavigated. Another way up would be from Blackcraig farm which gives a gentler ascent but does add to the distance at the end of the day or the other alternative is to reverse the walk.

Once on the top the going is easier with many cairns to follow. The summit cairn has an ordnance survey pillar but if in doubt it is easy enough to visit all the cairns on the top. The views from here are extensive moving from the Lowthers to the Rhinn of Kells to Arran and nearer at hand Blacklorg Hill.

There is a fence to Blacklorg which can be followed for a while but it wanders off round the side of the hill and over bog so it is best to take a southery bearing for Greenlorg, west of this area to avoid the peaty ground. There are remains of old fence posts going up this hill and to Blacklorg. To the west and below lies the Afton Reservoir opened in the 1950's and blending well with the surrounding countryside. Blacklorg's summit is rounded with a cairn and fence which follows up from the Kello Water, it is the Region fence and gives a guide all the way to Alhang, the next Donald.

The hillside can be described as rolling and grassy and as you walk beside the fence to Meikledodd Hill the entire walk almost unfolds. Here another fence comes up from Polskeoch (027683) on the Southern Upland Way. It gives a second possible route for this round but be warned the lower slopes are heavily forested.

The walking is easy on the whole with occasional bog at the cols, it is possible to walk round and avoid these areas but this does of course add on time and should be accounted for at the planning stage. Between Alwhat and Alhang the source of the Afton rises and from here excellent views of the reservoir can be seen. Alhang is soon taken and gives a good view of Windy Standard and its ordnance survey pillar.

Between here and Windy Standard there are two options: either a walk down by the fence to the marshy col or leave the fence and make a steep descent down to the Holm Burn where lumps of moraine can be seen. Whichever route is chosen sidle over to the col where three fences meet, one of which heads down to the Clennoch bothy. Walk on this westerly bearing if Cairnsmore of Carsphairn is to be climbed otherwise head south over Keoch Rig for Moorbrock.

Assuming the former is on the agenda then the descent and climb ahead is the biggest and hardest of the day. Once down follow the Bow Burn southwards towards the Gairy of Cairnsmore. Gairy is from the Gaelic word 'garbh' meaning rough so like Moorbrock, Beninner and the Blue Stones of Windy Standard indicates rocky areas and can be easily avoided. Above the gairy lies the top of Cairnsmore with its ordnance survey pillar and large summit cairn only a few metres away from a wall. The wall comes from Dunool and gives an alternative way to walk Cairnsmore of Carsphairn, which is also a Corbett. A walk along this ridge gives superb views of the Lowthers, the main Galloway Hills (the obvious one being the Merrick) and the Carsphairn Ridge, which you have just come over.

Walk down to the col between Beninner and Cairnsmore of Carsphairn and either continue to Beninner or take an easterly bearing for the watershed between Bow Burn and Poldores Burn. The ascent on this side is gentler and you are soon on Moorbrock's rounded summit where there are two small cairns, the summit one is just above Moorbrock Gairy. Views again are good of the surrounding area and show all too clearly the encroaching forestry up these hillsides.

From now on the bearing is northerly with Keoch Rig and another Alwhat (not named on the map) to be walked over before the fence followed earlier to Clennoch Bothy is regained. Once here keep beside it until the fence joins with the other two at the col. A couple of hundred metres from here is the Deil's Putting Stone worth a visit on the ascent up Windy Standard. It is a large grey boulder with a hollowed out bit on top suitable for the Devil to place his hand in for throwing, it also provides a good marker in mist. There is a fence up to the top of Windy Standard which despite living up to its name is a slightly disappointing hill, the fence though does not go to the ordnance survey pillar or the deserted weather station nearby but instead veers off to the east.

Again the views are good although trees appear to be steadily approaching the top, this time from the Carsphairn Forest. This is the last of the Carsphairn Donalds and now the way off can be seen.

Walk over Wedder Hill towards Lamb Hill and either down to the track which comes up between Lamb Hill and Black Hill; or cut down to the track which runs through the forest surrounding Afton Reservoir. Although the trees are thick there are ways through and on a windy day it gives shelter. The track then leads down to the dam followed by a tarred road to some rather out of place large buildings which are the waterworks. Keep on this road and you will finally arrive back at the start of the walk.

VERDICT: Although this is a long walk it can be broken into two by staying at Clennoch Bothy (which is basic) or by arranging transport at the other end. It is however worth the effort as it is a great walk with grand scenery and skies that stretch for miles in an area which is empty of other people.

View of the Afton Reservoir taken from the col between Alwhat and Alhang

The Galloway Hills

Taking a break at the loch between Meaul and Carlin's Cairn

The Author at the top of Carlin's Cairn

Beautiful Loch Skeen with White Coomb as a backdrop

Blackcraig Hill

Hexpeth Green path one way up to Windy Gyle

A splendid view down Glen Trool

A view point from Tinto

The frozen Games Hope Burn between Erie Hill and
Carlavin Hill on Route 1 (Moffat Hills)

The Galloway Hills

Route 1: "The Awful Hand"

O.S. MAP: Landranger Series 77.
                      Dalmellington to New Galloway.

DONALDS: (arranged in order walked)

NAME	HEIGHT	MAP REF.
Merrick	843m(2766ft)	428855
Kirriereoch Hill	786m(2565ft)	420871
Tarfessock	696m(2286ft)	409892
Shalloch on Minnoch	768m(2522ft)	407907

SUGGESTED STARTING POINT: NX 415805

COMPLETE ROUND: 19.5km/12 miles.

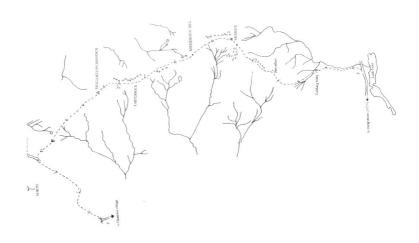

SIGHTS OF INTEREST: Bruce's Stone, Memorial to 'The Highway Man', Forest Nature Trails and Part of the Southern Upland Way.

NOTE: There is a good campsite at the west end of Loch Trool called Caldons. It is advantageous in the walk described to have transport available at the finish. Two of these hills (The Merrick and Shalloch on Minnoch) are Corbetts. The walk can be broken up into two or more walks, if so desired.

ROUTE: The best approach for this walk is from Bargrennan on the A714. From here follow the road past Glentrool village to Loch Trool where at the east end of the loch there is a car park (just below the Fell of Eschoncan). To the right of the car park on a small knoll stands Bruce's Monument.

It is a large boulder with the inscription: "In loyal remembrance of Robert the Bruce, King of Scots, whose victory in this glen over an English force in March, 1307, opened the campaign of independence, which he brought to a decisive close at Bannockburn on 24th June, 1314." This stone was erected for the 600th anniversary of Bruce's death.

From here there is a good view across Loch Trool to the battle site where Bruce is said to have lain in wait for Sir Aymer de Valences, Guardian of Scotland. Valences and 2,000 English troops passed in single file under Mulldonach and at this point Bruce gave the signal to set a huge pile of boulders in motion which crushed or drowned most of the English. This is known as the "Battle o' the Steps o' Trool" and took place in 1307. Walkers of the Southern Upland Way pass this spot on their way.

Opposite the stone is the starting point for the walk to the Merrick. A signposted path follows the west side of the Buchan burn to Culsharg bothy, now a ruin but once a shepherd's cottage. The path is not in good condition being rather boggy in places but, to compensate, the view southwards on a clear day is good. Above Culsharg it is time to leave the Glen Trool Forest behind and go onto open moor, there is still a path to follow which keeps beside a dyked wall to Benyellary, the Hill of the Eagle. This is the thumb of the 'Awful Hand' and at one time a Donald, it has a fine cairn.

The wall wanders around the side of the Merrick known as the Neive of the Spit and then according to the map stops. In fact as this is a popular walk a rough path continues to the top. The walking is easy over grassy slopes, but mist can easily come down and surround you very quickly in thick grey swirls. Should this happen a north easterly compass bearing will bring you to the ordanace survey pillar and large cairn there are also several large erratic boulders scattered around.

From the Merrick, which forms the index finger of the hand, a shapely ridge, known as the "Fang of Merrick" goes northwards to Kirriereoch Hill. On arrival at the cairn of Kirriereoch it is worthwhile looking back to get the best view of the Merrick. If the day is windy, cold, wet or misty escape for a while into a long cave that provides shelter and is found on the top of this summit.

Continue on a northerly bearing to travel down a steep broken slope to the col and then walk up Carmaddie Brae, westwards on the brae lie a collection of small lochans. It is a brae of ups and downs which finally terminates on the third Donald - Tarfessock. The summit is rough and stony with only a small cairn but it is a hill of interest to geologists for on the eastern side of the ridge is a line of pink rocks which contrast with the dark rock on the summit.

Shalloch of Minnoch forms the 'little finger' of the group and lies north of Tarfessock. By walking over the Nick of Carclach the top of Shalloch of Minnoch is soon reached. It is a slightly disappointing finish to a long day as it is a grassy mound, but three rivers (the Girvan, Stinchar and one of the sources of the Doon) start off from here, and views to the north west are good.

A descent down the Shalloch's northern slopes takes you back to the forestry track and hopefully transport at the Rowantree junction car park and viewpoint on the Straiton to Glentrool village road. Here, as at the start of the walk is another memorial stone, this time to David Bell, ' the Highway Man'. It consists of a cairn with a plaque on which is etched a relief map of the Galloway Hills and inscribed with the words "In remembrance of David Bell The Highway Man who knew these hills so well 1907 -1965." David Bell was a rough terrain cyclist, before mountain bikes were ever thought of, who wrote weekly articles about his travels around Galloway in the 'Ayrshire Post' for thirty years under the pen name of 'The Highway Man'.

VERDICT: One of the best areas for walking and although a popular walk there is still a feeling of remoteness. It is recommended that to do this walk you are fit and have a good knowledge of map and compass.

Robert the Bruce stone , Glentrool

The Galloway Hills

Route 2 "Rhinns of Kells"

O.S.MAP: Landranger Series 77.
                 Dalmellington to New Galloway.

DONALDS: (arranged in order walked)

NAME	HEIGHT	MAP REF.
Coran of Portmark	623m/2042ft	509937
Cairnsgarroch	659m/2155ft	515914
Meaul	695m/2280ft	501910
Carlin's Cairn	807m/2650ft	497884
Corserine	814m/2668ft	498871
(also a Corbett)		
Milldown	738m/2410ft	510839
Meikle Millyea	746m/2455ft	518829

SUGGESTED STARTING POINT: NX 553863

COMPLETE WALK: 24km/15miles plus 29km/18miles cycle ride

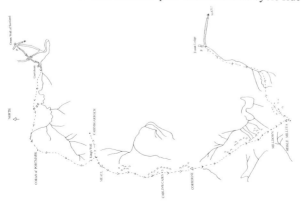

69

SIGHTS OF INTEREST: To the west lies the Silver Flowe, a National Nature Reserve, which covers about 191 ha and occupies the floor of the Cooran Lane between the Rhinns of Kells and Craignaw and Dungeon ranges. There are 7 bogs each characterised by a maze-like system of pools and when viewed from the hills above reflect the light, hence the description of "Silver Flowe". These bogs can be treacherous and should be walked round rather than through.

NOTES: A bothy, Blackhill of Bush (NX 481843) is found west of Millfire. It stands alone in a clearing surrounded by forestry midway between Loch Doon and Loch Trool.

The names Millyea and Milldown like many of the names in this area are corrupted gaelic being Meall Liath and Meall Doun respectively.

The Rhinns of Kells is one of four ranges in this area Merrick, Mullwharchar and the Lamachan hills are the others.

This is a long day if all the hills are to be walked so if transport can be arranged at both ends then it is an advantage. Alternative ways are by the local bus or by bike where the bike can be used to cycle to the start of the day and collected later.

ROUTE: Leave one vehicle at the car park of Forest Lodge where Norwegian names are found on forestry tracks to remind you that this forest was set up by a Norwegian shipping company. The road branches off the A713 north of St John's Dalry at Polharrow bridge (602844).

Return to this road and travel for 8 miles to the bridge at the Green Well of Scotland (NX 558945) past Carsphairn. This incidentally is also a starting point for Cairnsmore of Carsphairn. Turn left and follow the road to Garryhorn where the road becomes a track to the disused lead mines.

The building on the 300m contour line is the old school and stands beside a lovely tree where in spring daffodils dance in the breeze, the rest is desolation. Walk to the school and pass through a gate out onto the lower slopes of Knockower to make your way over to the col between this hill and the first Donald of the day, Coran of Portmark. It is easily ascended and gives ample reward of breathtaking views across to Loch Doon, the re-erected Doon Castle (removed to allow the loch to be extended), the small village of Craigmalloch and the head of the loch with the woods at Dinnis.

A fence shows the way over to Bow and Meaul. Follow this until a dyke joins the fence from the Lumps of Garryhorn. If the weather is clear then contour round to the col between Meaul and Cairnsgarroch to ascend this outlier otherwise follow the fence to Meaul and climb it first. Cairnsgarroch is worth going out to as from here you gain an idea of what lies ahead: Meaul, Carlin's Cairn, Corserine, Milldown and far off Meikle Millyea from Cairnsgarroch a descent down the ridge can also be made back to the starting point.

A well built dyke connects this hill with Meaul and in bad conditions can be followed up to the ordanace survey pillar on the summit. King's Well is passed on route. The story goes that Robert the Bruce, who at one time hid in this area, paused to drink from this water. At that time there were woods of oak, alder, willow, birch and hawthorn not the monotonous rows of dark green conifers. Not only does Meaul gives good views across to Shalloch of Minnoch and the Mullwharchar Range but you see down the entire length of Loch Doon.

Carlin's Cairn stands out the whole way round and now it is its turn to be climbed. The going is easy and just after Goat Craigs, at the col, are three small lochans useful on a hot day. However a map and compass is handy in mist as this is one of the areas when walking Donalds there are no fences or dykes to follow.

The first steep climb lies ahead but it is soon gained and the cairn that has tantalised from afar is reached. It lives up to its reputation of big. Originally this hill was a top of Corserine and did not gain Donald status until recently. How the cairn came to be so large is one of speculation but perhaps the miller's wife who came to Robert the Bruce's aid really did build it. Since then it has been added to and altered to provide many wind breaks for cold walkers.

Carlin's Cairn is the pivot point of the ridge and provides a good excuse for stopping before the steep descent and then haul up Corserine, a Corbett as well as a Donald, and possibly the least interesting part of the walk. The top of Corserine is flat and grassy although there are steep craggy faces to the north and east. At this point there are two ridges which cross each other and give Corserine its name. Other than an ordance survey pillar there is not much there but look down and westwards and you see acres of forest and the treacherous Silver Flowe bog glinting in the sunlight.

Those that wish to return to Forest Lodge from here can do so. Walk to the col between Corserine and Millfire and then descend east to Loch Minnoch. A track circuits Bennan Hill from here and arrives back at base. The col is also the point at which to leave for Black Bush Bothy, it is a long walk to the col from Corserine but a cairn shows that the low point has been reached. A funeral party carrying the wife of the shepherd from Black Bush had to leave the body here for several days during a terrible blizzard and left a pile of stones to mark the spot. There is now a further ascent to Millfire for those that continue.

Millfire is a top and marks a change in the geology of the ridge. It is a far more interesting walk over a number of crags and Milldown is soon reached. Shortly afterwards a descent down to the last col of the day appears. Newly planted conifers climb up the hillside and encroach on the ridge. Now Meikle Millyea stands ahead, the most southern of the major summits of this range. A boulder scramble gives interest to the walk up to the ordance survey pillar on the north end but there is a sting to the tail in that the south west top is the higher and requires a walk out and back to gain the peak.

Once returned to the pillar descend eastwards to Meikle Lump then down to the forest fence until a high style is found. Climb this and follow a fire break to the forest track which takes you back to the car park at Forest Lodge.

VERDICT: The whole ridge provides a superb day with a feast of views of the Galloway hills and beyond, however it is recommended that you are fit and can use the map and compass if need be. A day to savour in good weather.

Corserine, Meul and Cairnsgarroch part of the Rhinn of Kells

The Galloway Hills

Route 3 "The Dungeon Range"

O.S.MAP: Landranger Series 77.
Dalmellington to New Galloway.

DONALDS: (in order walked)

Name	Height	Map Ref.
Mullwharchar	692m/2270ft	454867
Dungeon Hill	616m/2020ft	461851
Craignaw	645m/2116ft	459833

SUGGESTED STARTING POINT: NX 415805

COMPLETE WALK: 20km/12½ miles.

SIGHTS OF INTERESTS: Bruce's Stone

NOTE: To the east of these hills lies the Silver Flowe.

The area is glacial and therefore of a rough nature. The time required to walk here is longer than might be suggested by the map.

If Craignaw is walked first then these hills can be combined with Merrick and Benyellary.

As the rock is granite and the area remote the Atomic Energy Authority showed interest in Mullwharchar in 1976 for geological research. So far the area is undisturbed and free from nuclear waste; enjoy the area while you can.

ROUTE: The start for this walk is the same as the Merrick round, that is from the Glen Trool car park and The Bruce Memorial Stone.

Take the untarred road to Glenhead by descending past the Memorial Stone to cross the Buchan Burn by the Earl of Galloway's or Buchan Bridge. A sign points the way over a style at the end of the natural oak woodland. This goes diagonally to a dyke on the side of Buchan Hill and thence to the Gairland Burn. Height is gained unknowingly and superb views of Glen Trool are seen.

The valley of the Gairland Burn is a hanging valley and soon hides Glen Trool. There is already a feeling of remoteness with the beauty of the woods being replaced by the ruggedness of the glacial surroundings. The burn is followed up to Loch Valley and stretches eastwards with scenery unfolding with every step.

The slightly boggy path continues up to the next of this complicated series of lochs - Loch Neldricken. Where the path officially ends on the map, are a row of stepping boulders easily crossed under normal conditions but which on occasions can be submerged and that is warning for the return journey.

Each loch is different and if possible grander than the last but all have appeared by glacial action. Loch Neldricken is almost cut in two by a finger of land pointing south. West of this is the ' Murder Hole' made famous by Crockett in 'The Raiders' and said never to freeze in winter. Walk by the side of this beautiful loch with Meaul beside you, past the 'Murder Hole' and through a narrow cleft between Ewe Rig and Rig of Loch Enoch to Loch Arron, the smallest of these four lochs.

The way ahead is an impressive pass between Craig Neldricken and Redstone Rig to Loch Enoch with its white sands. These granite sands were once famed for their sharpness by knife grinders and can still cut bare feet. Stories are told of fish in these lochs with truncated fins due to this very sharpness.

74

To walk up to this loch alone is worth every footstep, however the range which has enticed on the way now confronts. Mullwharchar stares down from the north of the loch and the decision to walk by the east or the west of the loch is yours. The easiest way is perhaps by the east to where the Pulskaig Burn runs through the pass to the Gala Lane, a river flowing into Loch Doon. The climb although steep is easy onto Mullwharchar's boulder top and the views are superb. Down Loch Doon Arran can be seen in the distance, over to the east the Rhinns of Kells, closer lies the Merrick Range and the pimple of Dungeon Hill with craggy Craignaw behind. Here the scenery is rough and reminds one of the Highlands in miniature. There are no fences to follow and underfoot rough tussock grass, bog and heather can hold you back.

Return to the col and move over boggy ground towards Dungeon Hill. The grass on this side soon turns out to have granite pavements, slabs and boulders scattered as the ice left them on the top. Sit at the cairn and look over the silver glint of the Flowe and three small lochs below with the rise of forestry creeping up Corserine and Milldown. The small Black Bush bothy looks forlorn amongst so much green.

Before leaving the top a visit to the Devils' Bowling Green will provide further fascination. It lies north of the summit on the north west summit known as Wee Craignaw. It is a massive level area covered with erratic boulders left by the ice sheets. Legend has it that the Devil and Pan were hungry and both wished to eat the nearby loaf of bread. To settle the argument they agreed to a game of bowls but the game ended in battle and the rocks were flung far and wide making the 'Murder Hole' and the loch within a loch on Loch Enoch. The 'Loaf of Bread' is not so easily detected but lies some hundred metres or so to the north east of the summit.

Directly south is the rock face of Craignaw with a long sheer drop. The sensible route is west skirting Craignairny to the cairn which marks the Nick of the Dungeon or the col between Dungeon and Craignaw. This last part of the walk is enjoyable for the way ahead is over boulders and easy crags to the top where at last the Silver Flowe is finally seen in all its fascinating glory. Light reflected at all angles produces an unbelievable shimmering effect.

The obvious descent from the summit is by a burn in a grass gully down to Loch Neldricken. As you start a memorial to two American Air Force Captains is seen. The plaque reads :

"In loving memory
of
Capt R.A. Hetzner 28 USAF
Capt R.C. Spalding 30 USAF
F1- 11E CREW
Crashed Dec. 1979
AKHWC"

Further evidence is seen in wreckage still there and the more permanent white scar on the opposite side of the gully.

Once the southern shores are reached walk south west towards the stepping stones seen at the start of the day and head down the same path back to the busy car park.

VERDICT: This is perhaps my favourite walk of the entire Donalds but it requires a certain stamina and knowledge of the hills. Savour it on a fine day when fit.

View of Loch Doon from Dungeon Hill

The Galloway Hills

Route 4 "The Minnigaff Hills"

O.S.MAP: Landranger Series 77.
Dalmellington to New Galloway.

DONALDS: (in order walked)

Name	Height	Map Ref.
Larg Hill	675m/2216ft	425757
Lamachan Hill	716m/2350ft	435770
Curleywee	674m/2212ft	454769
Millfore	656m/2151ft	478755

SUGGESTED STARTING POINT: NX 448705

COMPLETE WALK: 22km/14miles.

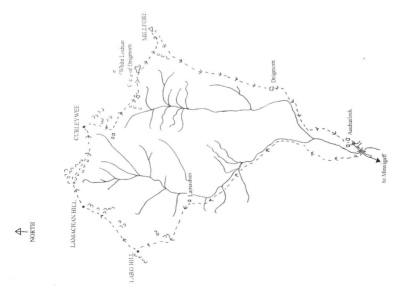

77

SIGHTS OF INTERESTS: To the south of Millfore is Murray's Monument. This is a monument in memory to Alexander Murray born at Dunkitterick. He was the Professor of Oriental Languages at Edinburgh University for a year prior to his death in 1813.

There is also a wild goat park at this spot and the Galloway deer museum, forest walks and drives can be found at Clatteringshaws Loch.

Near the Caldons camp-site is the walled structure known as the Martyrs Tomb. It was erected in memory of several Covenanters who were surprised at prayer at this spot.

NOTES: This horseshoe has some access problems at the start of the walk due to forestry so if a break is spotted it is worth walking up it.

There is a bothy at White Laggan on Loch Dee and the Southern Upland Long Distance footpath passes Loch Dee.

It is a rugged area and time must be taken into account for this type of terrain especially between Curleywee and Millfore where there is a steep descent to the path at the col and then a fairly strenuous ascent up to the summit. Care of course must also be taken in poor weather as navigation can be tricky.

ROUTE: This line of hills, unlike the other three walks, lies across the map on a west/east line and is more of a horseshoe than a long range of hills. This means no transport problems and a plus in that it can be walked without retracing steps.

Take the road to Auchinleck beside the Penkiln Burn and start from the bridge just before Auchinleck House. To reach this road go to Minnigaff (NX 412663) near Newton Stewart on the A714. The road goes past the Indoor Bowling Rink in Minnigaff and follows the east side of the burn.

Follow the forestry track, which starts at the bridge, to the ruins of Lamachan. Large areas of this forest have been cleared due to felling and wind damage giving slightly easier access than in the past. However it is wise to make sure any fire break goes out onto the hillside, otherwise it is possible to go round in circles or become blocked off.

Leave the track just before the Lamachan ruins and head to the dyke which runs to Larg's summit. Once out of the forest it is a pleasant walk over short grass to the top - the actual cairn is slightly west of the dyke and is small for locating in mist. The dyke is a convenient marker to the col where it then descends down towards Mulmein Moss and Caldons Campsite. Remains of an old fence show the way up Lamachan Hill the highest of the four hills. The grass provides good grazing for sheep and wild goats which are often seen here.

At the summit of Lamachan there is no real cairn but a metal post encircled by the remains of a dyke. Another wall joins this from the west beside Caldons Burn. Not only can the steep crags of Curleywee be seen from here but the whole circuitous route can be mapped out on the ground. Good views are also revealed over Glen Trool and the Merrick hills.

Curleywee is a rough hill something similar to Arthur's Seat in Edinburgh, with its classical shape it is certainly one of the most impressive hills in this area. The ascent is a rewarding scramble and the views are splendid. At least eight lochs can be seen, the Silver Flowe, the Merrick, Dungeon and Kells ranges are all there with panoramas even further afield.

To get to Curleywee go eastwards from Lamachan following the old fence posts to Bennanbrack where the posts with a well trodden path turn sharp right and go downwards. The ground undulates over two small bumps but ahead lies a dyke blocking the way at the col. Cross this and make your way to the foot of a steep haul over scree and crags to the narrow summit of Curleywee and a small cairn.

The next part of the walk can be tricky, especially if mist is around. It involves a steep descent down to a col between Curleywee and Bennan Hill, where a small lochan (NX 453764) can be used as a marker. From here a further descent to the pass between Loch Dee and Auchinleck is made. The ground underfoot changes to moss and bog as height is lost. A return to the start on the path along the Pulnee Burn southwards may be taken at this point if you do not wish to continue to Millfore.

This pass is the low point of the walk. Ahead lies a slightly circuitous route to the Black Loch and then to the White Lochan of Drigmore, where curlers once gathered and a small building was erected. It is a large sheet of water for this level and another good marker in mist. A direct compass bearing from here would take you to the top of Millfore. On a fine day it is possible to angle round the ridge to Millfore's summit and ordnance survey pillar.

Once the top is gained the way you have come can be traced just as earlier from Larg Hill the way ahead could be followed. It looks impressive with the deep cleft between Curleywee and Lamachan showing up clearly. To the east is the large sheet of water which is Clatteringshaws Loch.

Walk along the ridge to Drigmorn Hill where a prominent cairn is seen and then down gentle slopes to Drigmorn Farm. A track winds back through forestry to Auchinleck farm and shortly back to the bridge and the starting point.

VERDICT: One of the few walks in the Donalds which is almost a horseshoe. A pleasant walk but in poor conditions can give tricky navigation. The other problem is forestry and ways through this may cause problems.

Curleywee and Lamachan Hill from Mullwharcher

The Galloway Hills

Route 5: Cairnsmore of Fleet

O.S.MAP: Landranger Series 83
Newton Stewart & Kirkcudbright area.

DONALD:

Name	Height	Map Ref.
Cairnsmore of Fleet	711m/2331ft	502671

SUGGESTED STARTING POINT: NX 470640

COMPLETE WALK: 10 km/6 miles.

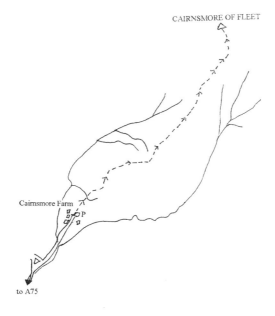

SIGHTS OF INTERESTS: Cairnsmore of Fleet is a Nature Reserve run by the Nature Conservancy Council and is now the only site in the District to include unafforested ground through an altitude range of 167m up to the summit height of 711m. It is important for the upland red deer, feral goat, golden plover and raven.

Nearby is Creetown where there is an interesting gem museum. Forest walks abound in this area as do castles.

ROUTE: This hill dominates the eastern side of Newton Stewart and the river Cree. One of the easier ascents is from the A 75 Newton Stewart to Dumfries road.

Take the unclassified road to Cairnsmore Farm from Muirfad (NX 457630) about 7km south from Newton Stewart. The road goes under an old railway viaduct to Cairnsmore Farm where there is a car park and picnic spot. This is the start of the walk.

A gate beside the car park opens into a field walk diagonally from here to another gate at the opposite end of the field. Go through this then cross a style into Bardroch Wood with Crammery Hill to the east of you. A path takes you all the way up (about half way up the path there is a forestry track to cross).

The wood terminates with a fence and another stile to climb over and now you are onto open hillside. The path is slightly steep to begin with but soon levels out once on the ridge and by now many small cairns show the way to the top. Superb views are revealed out over Wigtown Sands to the south, north east is the Nature Reserve and Meikle Mulltaggart, the Galloway Hills and Mull of Galloway.

The summit of Cairnsmore of Fleet is soon reached where there is a memorial to six aeroplanes and their crews, some of the many planes which have crashed on this hill over the years (the area is often misty which might account for this high number). The cairn is large and nearby is the remains of a small building and an ordnance survey pillar. There is no fence to follow on this hill but the path is fairly well defined.

The return can be by the same way or the walk can be continued over Meikle Mulltaggart to Little Mulltaggart then eventually pick up a footpath over Knocktim but the way can be boggy.

VERDICT: This is a short walk but enjoyable giving great views.

The broad hill of Cairnsmore of Fleet

The Roxburgh Hills

The Roxburgh Hills

O.S.MAP: Landranger Series 79.
Hawick & Eskdale area.

DONALD:

Name	Height	Map Ref.
Cauldcleuch Head.	610m/2,028ft	461008

SUGGESTED STARTING POINT: NT476967

COMPLETE WALK: 13km/8½ miles.

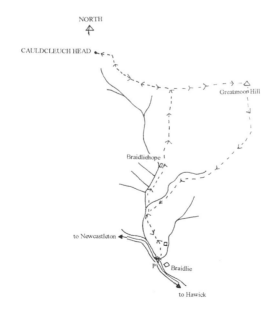

SIGHTS OF INTEREST: The castle is well worth a visit. Nearby is the imposing ruin of Hermitage Castle once the strength of Liddesdale. The castle has a long and cruel history and was the stronghold at various times of the Soulis, Dacre, Douglas and Bothwell families. Throughout the centuries the castle and the surrounding hills saw violent deeds recorded in ballad and story but there was romance here too. In 1566 James Hepburn, Earl of Bothwell, lay severely wounded at the castle and was visited by Mary Queen of Scots. She had travelled over the hills and bogs from Jedburgh, a journey of over fifty miles.

NOTE: This hill can also be walked in conjunction with Tudhope Hill to the west, which makes a pleasant round.

ROUTE: The best access to Cauldcleuch lies at the bridge over the Hermitage water to New Bradlie, a neat and tidy Border farm, about a mile west from Hermitage Castle on the connecting road between the A 7 and B 6399 south of Hawick.

Set off beside wooded banks of alder, birch and hazel with glimpses of brown water through the trees. Cross the bridge where a gate opens easily and leads to a forked track the right branch of which goes to the farm. Take the left branch and go through some fields where cattle often graze. The track's high point is edged with rowans and hawthorn before it plunges down to the burn and it is necessary to ford the various offshoots of the main stream as you walk along.

Go past Braidleehope, a cottage which still has a good slate roof although inside it is in ruins and used by sheep for shelter. Leave the ruin behind to climb the path to steeper ground where the path disappears. The Braidlee stream below becomes the Crib burn to the west and the Barley burn to the east as they fork round the ground known as the Queen's Mire. This is the spot where Queen Mary, on returning from Hermitage Castle, almost sunk into the bog from which she and her horse were extricated from with great difficulty. Now the bog is mainly rough pasture which supports the sheep.

The round top of Cauldcleuch Head can be seen quite clearly. The grass sides are scarred with animal tracks and worn through to the red soil in other parts. The Crib burn drains out of the summit and its course can be followed but the best policy is to walk to the tree line in the distance along the ridge known as Windy Edge. There are quite often electric fences in this area so care must be taken.

The climb is gentle to Windy Edge where to the north lie vast tracks of neatly planted forest contained by a well maintained fence. Follow the fence westwards to the summit and Cauldcleuch is soon reached. Whortleberries may provide a meal as you walk over the thick tussock grass, bog cotton and peat hag but time must be allowed for this type of vegetation. The top may be slightly disappointing as it is flat with only a strainer post anchored in bog to indicate the top. There is of course little in the way of shelter or comfort for a lunch site but to the south there are views of the

Solway Firth and Criffel stands in silhouette. Smoke from four large concrete towers can be seen as can the high peaks of the Lake District.

If you turn to the east the Cheviots form a natural wall between two nations. The north shows the gentler Moorfoots and the Tweedsmuir hills; closer still are the Eildons under which according to legend lies King Arthur and his knights, ready to rise again to defend their country at the call of a bugle. Not only are the views good but Cauldcleuch also has the privilege of being the most easterly hill of over 2,000ft in Scotland.

A concrete ordnance survey pillar stands out on Tudhope Hill, a mile or so to the west, and if transport is arranged makes a good round otherwise retrace your steps back along Windy Edge to Swire Knowe, the col between Cauldcleuch Head and Greatmoor Hill. At the col is the continuation of the track which brought you up. It can be seen wandering through the forestry down to Priesthaugh and again offers an alternative way to these hills from that side. It is an old track being part of the route followed by Queen Mary on her epic journey. From here either return by the track to the start or extend the walk by going over Greatmoor Hill.

The forestry fence goes up past Starcleugh Edge, a small bump on the horizon and a convenient sheep track beside the fence helps avoid the taller tussock grass. The grass is better cropped on this side and many sheep with lambs are seen here in Spring.

Greatmoor top, although lower than Cauldcleuch, is more like a top should be. It is flat with some rock and lacks peat hag. There is a well built cairn offering some shelter with an ordnance survey pillar, balancing the one on Tudhope, which at 599m/1,966ft is strangely the same height as Greatmoor.

Two possibilities of descent can be seen below either by way of the path to the Barley burn and so back to Braidleehope, or by higher ground. Weather conditions will be the decisive factor but the view along the ridge is good. If keeping to the ridge descend from the top down a grassy slope to Ready Edge you can then descend anywhere from here. The Tongue burn is a good spot to head for and will take you back to the track and so to the start.

VERDICT: Although this walk is short in comparison to some of the other days it is well worth walking for the views and the lack of people. However it is worth checking access with the farmer in the lambing season.

Meeting of fences at the top of Cauldcleuch

The Cheviot Hills

The Cheviot Hills

Route 1

O.S. MAP: Landranger Series maps 74 and 80.
Kelso and Cheviot Hills & Kielder Forest.

DONALD:

NAME	HEIGHT	MAP REF.
Windy Gyle	619m(2034ft)	855152.

SUGGESTED STARTING POINT: NT 852188

COMPLETE ROUND: 16km/10 miles.

NORTH

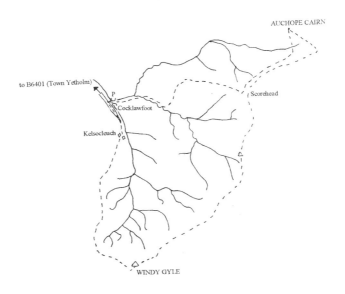

SIGHTS OF INTEREST: Windy Gyle has one of the largest cairns in the Cheviots. It was probably a prehistoric burial place for chiefs who dwelt in the Bronze Age period but it is also known as Russell's Cairn. Lord Russell was the son-in-law of Sir John Forster of Bamburgh Castle, the English Warden of the Middle Marches. His opposite number was Kerr of Fernihirst, who disliked the English intensely especially Russell. The meeting of the Marches could be explosive affairs and the meeting of July the 27th.1585 was no exception. During the truce, disputes between both sides were dealt with as fairly as possible while in the background stalls and the like would be set up giving a holiday atmosphere. On this occasion a quarrel broke out amongst the bystanders and an English lad was caught stealing a pair of spurs. The wardens and their assistants wisely chose to continue and ignore the disturbance, but Lord Russell, already a marked man from an incidence occurring some ten years previously, went to inquire into the matter. An unidentified Scot shot him and mortally wounded him. All there helped to bury him and this cairn is said to mark the spot. Whether this is what actually happened is difficult to say, but it is an interesting tale and one worth contemplating while sitting in the shelter provided.

NOTE: Windy Gyle is not the highest of the six hills which form the Cheviots and Auchope Cairn at 726m/2382ft is but a top of Cheviot itself. However both are of some interest in that they sit astride the National Boundary of Scotland and England and offer a pleasant circular walk with superb views and the challenge of walking part of the Pennine Way.

Part of the Pennine Way is very eroded therefore time must be taken into account for the extra effort involved in these walking conditions. However, recently flagstones have been laid along most parts of the route and have helped improved walking conditions.

ROUTE: A car can be parked at the end of the metalled road beside Cocklawfoot. This is reached by a single track road off the B6401 to Town Yetholm at Primsidemill (NT 813266) and runs southwards through the Bowmont valley to give a delightful start to the day.

There is a choice of ascents but to get the most out of the day walk along to Kelsocleugh farm for a short distance and then make your way to the forestry plantation behind the farm, a stile goes over the dyke and there is a way over the grass fields. Once past the plantation another gate gives access onto Kelsocleugh Rig. The going is easy with a grassy path to follow to Windy Rig. By now the long distance footpath is obvious. It has come from Byrness some 21km away and continues to Town Yetholm some 21km in the other direction. It is well trodden and a fence also marks the way up to Windy Gyle.

The top is easily recognised by the enormous cairn with a metal star shaped marker known as Lord Russell's Cairn. There are many shelters round the cairn - needed as the hill is aptly named for there always seems to be a wind. From this spot turn towards Cheviot and walk gently downhill passing another small cairn in memorial to another who died as recently as 1988. Stay on the Scottish side of the fence for the going is easier, as is to be expected with most long distance paths, increased human traffic has put pressure on the terrain and ground at one time covered by heather, moss and tussock grass has now become waterlogged in stretches, even in dry conditions. In the last ten or so years much of this area now has flagstones flown in by helicopter.

Pause at the third cairn 1.5km along from Windy Gyle with green flaking post and look down at Cocklawridge and a green drove road coming from Cocklawfoot. This provides another route up to Windy Gyle, or down, if a short day is planned. Southwards this road continues to Alwinton, it was an old crossing known at one time as the Hexpethgate and used for access from and to Cocklaw from the English side.

At this point too the Pennine Way crosses to the English side of the fence to continue onto King'Seat and then to Scorehead (or Crookedside Head). From here the climb is steep for at least a kilometre and heads towards a prominent rock outcrop. This land mark, the Hanging Stone, at one time marked the start of the East Marches and the end of the Middle Marches. Now the boundary follows the watershed and is about a hundred metres to the west, a change which occurred in the 16th century but up to this date the stone was jointly owned by both countries. Its curious name, dating from medieval times, relates to the forward tilt of the broken rock which projects over the more solid rock underneath. Legend though, tells of a pedlar, who passing the rock, accidentally hanged himself by the strap of his pack which had slipped down round his neck.

A spot height of 743m on the map marks a right angled turn of the Border fence to the north west. From here Cheviot may be climbed otherwise continue beside the fence to Auchope Cairn over an extremely boggy area. Auchope Cairn is a well built cairn with the summit overlooking the Hen Hole, a well known feature of the approach to Cheviot from the College Burn side in the past this inspiring gash was used for hiding stolen cattle by the local character Black Jack, a reiver, today it is used by rock climbers.

The Pennine Way continues along the Border fence towards the Schill and then to Kirk Yetholm. So unless transport is arranged walk back to Cocklawfoot by contouring round Scorehead and then down to Mallie Side (451m), here a steep drop down brings you to King's Seat burn. Then follow the landrover track passing green fields to a bridge over the river and so to the start.

VERDICT: A longer walk than suggested by the distance because of underfoot conditions. However it is a pleasant walk and offers a chance to walk along one of the wilder parts of the Pennine Way.

Russell's Cairn at the top of Windy Gyle

The Cheviot Hills (England's 2,000 Footers.)

Route 2

O.S. MAP: Landranger Series 74 and 80.

Kelso and Cheviot Hills & Kielder Forest area.

DONALDS: (in order walked)

NAME	HEIGHT	MAP REF.
The Cheviot	815m(2676ft)	909205
Cairn Hill	776m(2546ft)	903196
Comb Fell	650m(2160ft)	919187
Hedgehope Hill	714m(2348ft)	944197

SUGGESTED STARTING POINT: NT 949220

COMPLETE ROUND: 18km /11 miles.

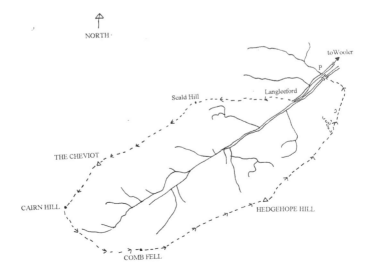

SIGHTS OF INTEREST: These hills lie in part of the Northumberland National Park which stretches from the Cheviot Hills to the Roman Wall. This area has for centuries formed a physical barrier between Scotland and England and despite being a National Park remains isolated and relatively unknown.

Wooler is a small market town and forms a convenient base for exploring the Cheviot Hills, nearby is the ancient town of Berwick-upon-Tweed.

On Cheviot when conditions are exceptionally dry parts of a Stirling and an Anson can be seen, both crashed in 1944.

NOTES: Alternative routes are also possible either by combining Cheviot and Cairn Hill in the walk with Windy Gyle or taking in Comb Fell and Hedgehope Hill with the Cushat Law and Bloodybush Edge day. The complete round is also possible with a start from Hartside to Cushat Law returning from Hedgehope by the Linhope Spout Waterfall - this round is long and arduous.

ROUTE: Leave Wooler by Cheviot Street pass the Youth Hostel to turn first right to Earle then follow the sign posts to Langleeford. Park the car by the bridge where public access ends.

The Cheviots were formed by volcanic action many millions of years ago, now they are worn down to rounded summits which have steep sides and deep valleys still relatively clear of forestry so the start for the walk can take place anywhere from the bridge. However there is a signposted route which leads to the large bulk of Cheviot over relatively easy ground. There are styles over fences, and the route has marker posts to follow.

Scald Hill is first ascended and then a path follows a fence through badly eroded peat. Cheviot swells upwards with almost no gradient and the summit plateau is virtually a bog. It is worth quoting here an extract on Cheviot from the first S.M.C. journal written in 1890; "When you have jumped and floundered through it for over a mile, you arrive at a sort of an island in the morass, surmounted by a few stakes and numerous broken bottles. Such is the top of Cheviot!" Nothing much has changed except there is now an ordnance survey pillar slightly north of the actual fence and flagstones have also recently been laid over the worst of the bog So be warned the best times to visit this hill is either during a drought or in winter, when the ground is either hard or frozen.

Take a south westerly bearing over more peat hag from here to join part of the Pennine Way which goes to Cairn Hill at the head of the Harthope Valley. Pass over this and then bear off to the south east heading towards Comb Fell. The going now becomes slightly easier in that there is less exposed peat hag and more grassy tussocks, heather and cloudberry. Comb Fell is a featureless mound but it forms a good view-point this time for Scald Hill, Cheviot and Auchope Cairn.

Turn north east with the fence on your right to walk on easier ground (although it can be hard going due to the amount of peat hag and bog). There is a small descent with a climb up a steeper section to the fine summit of Hedgehope in many ways grander than the higher Cheviot. The grounds falls away steeply and on its summit is a large cairn with shelter and a three fence junction. From here are long distant views of the Northumberland coast and the islands; Cheviot and Cairn Hill fill the landscape to the north west, north are the Lammermuirs and to the south on a clear day Skiddaw can be seen.

From the top of Hedgehope take a bearing north east for Long Crags and Housey Crags (NT 958218I). It is now downhill most of the way over grass and heather (there is a fence which goes downwards but it is not worth following as it surrounds the forest to the south east of the crags). If you enjoy a scramble then the crags give you an excuse to stop for a while before following a path down over gentle grassy slopes to a bridge over a small stream, the popular picnic area and your vehicle.

VERDICT: The walk is strenuous involving a walk over some rather large peat bogs which can be extremely tiring when wet, time therefore can vary with conditions underfoot.

Cheviot from Hedgehope

The Cheviot Hills (ENGLAND'S 2,000 Footers.)

Route 3

O.S. MAP: Landranger Series 80 and 81.

   Cheviot Hills & Kielder Forest area and

   Alnwick, Morpeth & surrounding area.

DONALDS: (in order walked)

NAME	HEIGHT	MAP REF.
Cushat Law	616m(2020ft)	928137
Bloodybush Edge	610m(2001ft)	902144

SUGGESTED STARTING POINT: NT 977162

COMPLETE ROUND: 20km/12½ miles.

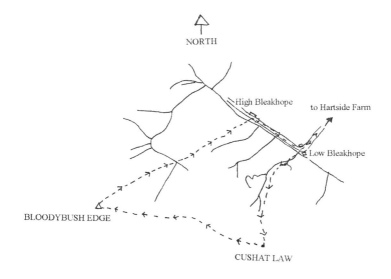

97

SIGHTS OF INTEREST: There is a small information centre at Ingram run by the Northumberland National Park. The church here dates from the 12th.century and the strong tower and narrow windows suggest it was originally used for defence. The font (1662) shows the Percy crescent on several of its faces.

Hill top camps dating back to the British tribes of long ago.

Nearby is Linhope Spout. This is a well known beauty spot and rather a lovely waterfall. It falls straight into a deep pool from a height of 15m. When the burn is in full spate the waterfall is an impressive sight.

NOTE: These hills lie in part of the Northumberland National Park. Routes from Alwinton are also possible.

These two hills lie south of Cheviot and provide an enjoyable days walk, if so inclined they can be included with Windy Gyle and then continue round the Cheviot Round to give a very long strenuous day. There is a drop of 351m at Uswayford with a corresponding ascent up to the Hexpethgate drove road at the other side to consider if this route is walked.

ROUTE: Take the A697 road south out of Wooler and turn right at the Brandon White Hotel to Ingram and Linhope. This is the valley of the river Breamish and gives a pleasant introduction to Northumberland's National Park. At Hartside farm the road becomes private but there is adequate room to park the car and a variety of walks opens up. To get to Cushat Law and Bloodybush Edge take the left hand road to Alnhammoor. The road is tarred and goes past Meggrim's Knowe beside the Breamish to Low and High Bleakhope, two rather remote farms.

On arrival at Low Bleakhope follow the Hareshaw Cleugh up to Cushat Law sometimes called the 'Monarch of Kidland' or the 'Hill of the Woodpigeons'. The going is steady over tussock grass and heather mounds to the round top. A cairn marks the summit and the view over to Hedgehope Hill, Cheviot and nearer Bloodybush Edge give an excuse for a breather. Below is Kidland Forest, no doubt where the woodpigeons are to be found. To the south of the forest are vast tracks set aside for military use.

A fence goes to the col and up to the ordnance survey pillar which is the only distinctive feature of Bloodybush Edge. There is no bush, blood or edge - just a round hill whose name in fact is said to record some long forgotten battle. The fence runs beside peat hags and goes down to a forestry plantation, so instead of following this, descend over rough ground to High Bleakhope (NT 926158). Then follow the track to Low Bleakhope and the road back to your starting point.

VERDICT: A pleasant walk over rough but firm ground.

View from Cushat Law

Information about Percy Donald

Personal Details: Born in Edinburgh on the 18th January 1892 to Mrs and Mr Isaac Donald. His father was a journalist.

Donald died in 1938 whilst in the hills he loved.

Percy Donald was known as a man of strong character with an eye for meticulous detail and enjoyed the challenge of neatly arranging statistical facts.

Donald was a boy scout and in later years was to become the official photographer for the Edinburgh Troops.

School Career: His primary years were at Miss Sidney's Private School. He then attended George Watson's Boys School between the years of 1903 and 1908.

University Career: He matriculated at Edinburgh University in 1909 where he took an engineering degree. He graduated on the 29th March as a Bachelor of Science.

Army Record: During the First World War Donald served as an engineer's assistant with Rly. (Railway) Coy., R.N.D. (The Royal Navy Division) – a division formed only in the First World War, in the 1st Field Company Division as a sapper or private, in 1916 with the Royal Engineers as a temporary second lieutenant, in 1918 as assistant captain.

He was also at Gallipoli in 1915 and in France between 1916 to 1919 at Arras, Ypres and Cambrai.

Climbing Career: He joined the Scottish Mountaineering Club in 1922 and served on the committee from 1925 to 1928. He was Custodian of Slides and during this time he reorganised the slide collection utilising his eye for perfection of detail. Donald was regarded as an expert photographer and was asked to rewrite the article on photography for the republished S.M.C. 'General Guidebook' in 1933. During this time he also contributed many photographs to the journal.

When the CIC hut was built Donald was asked to be in charge of all the equipment.

Donald regularly attended the S.M.C. meets but he was not a rock climber being happiest hill walking and exploring hill streams either alone or with a few friends. There is no known record of Donald completing the Munros.

In 1935 Percy Donald published in the S.M.C. journal an article titled 'The Two Thousand Tops of the Scottish Lowlands'. These became known as 'The Donalds'.

Bibliography

Barnett Border By-Ways and lothian lore Robert Grant & Son

Clavering (1953) From The Border Hills Thomas Nelson & Sons Ltd.

Crockett S.R. 1904 Raiderland Hodder & Stoughton

McBain J. The Merrick and the Neighbouring Hills Stephen & Pollock, Ayr

Macleod Innes Discovering Galloway

S.M.C JOURNALS

VOL XX The Two-Thousand Feet tops of the Scottish Lowlands Percy Donald.

VOL IX The Lowther Hill and Queensberry

VOL XXII The Lowther Hills J.Rooke Corbett

VOL I The Highlands of Galloway Colin B.Philip

VOl II Galloway and Ayrshire Hills H.B.Watt

VOL XXI The Galloway Hills John Dow

VOL XXV Back Bearings on Merrick Ian W Craig

VOL IV Peebles to St.Mary's Loch by Glen Sax

VOL I Minchmoor W.Douglas

VOL I A Day on the Moffat Hills W. Cowan

VOL XXIII The Peeblesshire Hills W.L.Coats

VOL II Andrewhinnie Hill Prof.Veitch

VOL I The Cheviot

VOL XXII Notes on the Cheviot Hills

VOl XXII Additional Notes on Cheviot Hills

VOL XX Tinto Hills

VOL XXI The Tinto Indicator by J.A. Parker.

MAGAZINES

Scottish Field April 1966 'The Galloway Diamond ' K.M.Andrew.

　　　　　March 1968 'High and Low in Galloway' Tom Weir.

Scots Magazine April 1961 'Days on the Awful Hand' K.M.Andrew.

　　　　　Dec. 1966 'Taming High Galloway' Benington Marsh